The Reds Remembered

Hannah Barbara Ann Moore, Trudy Kate Beckett-McInroy,
Phoebe Evangeline Beckett-McInroy and Imogen Nicola Moore

DEDICATION

We dedicate this book to our Grandad, who has shared so many stories and words of wisdom with us over the years. We thank you for throwing us into bushes, trying to ride a scooter at 70++, singing in supermarkets and acting the 'goat' teaching us your daughters' quirky dances! We hope you like 'The Reds Remembered' - we won't forget them!

The Reds Remembered

Preface

Countless books have been written about English football, the beautiful game. Many of those have extolled the years in the fifties and sixties, the decades which covered the emergence of Manchester United's famous Busby Babes. The club itself has attracted writers by the legion, stretching well before the fifties and up to the present day.

Very few, if any, have been able to show insights from a player who wore the Reds shirt at the same time as Matt Busby's prodigies. This book, The Reds Remembered, is laden with memories, reflections, opinions and stories from Terry Beckett. As a young, homebred Mancunian from the inner-city district of Ancoats, Terry filled the right wing and inside-right slots for the club at academy and youth and team levels. He lived, trained and worked alongside all of those who perished in the Munich air disaster in 1958.

This book does not focus exclusively on that tragedy, but includes it alongside the story of Terry's own career progression in the game, as well as remarkably unique, close-up vignettes on celebrated team mates, coaches and managers of that era. As a talent scout for the Reds for more than thirty years, the longevity of his association with the club is unmatched.

We, his four granddaughters, decided as a family project to have a series of interviews with Grandad to let him share his treasure trove of football knowledge.

Much of the results of these form the foundation of **The Reds Remembered**.

Hannah Barbara Ann Moore, Trudy Kate Beckett-McInroy,
Phoebe Evangeline Beckett-McInroy and Imogen Nicola Moore

CONTENTS

ACKNOWLEDGMENTS

We wish to thank Seumas Gallacher for his support in editorial and diligent fact checking, and Janie Parks for her patience and design work.

1 THE EARLY DAYS

In the final years of the nineteen-thirties, the Second World War loomed across Europe. In the industrial northwest of the United Kingdom, the inner city of Collyhurst in Manchester replicated other large urban centres across the country. Money was scarce. The lot of the ordinary working man was more than filled with the need to keep a job, any job, in order to feed their families. The constant influx of migrants, such as the Irish and Italian, fed into the gritty, down-to-earth communities already firmly planted in the city.

The economic decline through the decade impacted severely on the textile giants which had been for so long the bedrock of the region's commerce. Unemployment spread a dark shadow over the north as work became scarcer and scarcer.

Into this backdrop of hardship, Terrence Joseph Beckett was born in October, 1938, to parents, Sam and Kate. The boy knew little of the passage of the war itself, being barely six years old when the hostilities ceased in 1945.

Terry Beckett with his mother Kate Beckett

What he does remember is one of the many evenings when the German bombers came calling over the city. For whatever reason, his father decided they were not going to move to the air raid shelter that night. The sound of the explosions nearby was terrifying and Terry recalls hiding under a blanket to try to muffle the noise.

Every time thereafter, the family sought the shelter like everyone else.

Physically, the lad was not overly big, but his wiry frame housed a talent for football. Many thousands of other boys competed week after week on the playing fields in and around Greater Manchester. Only a handful reached the upper levels of the game professionally. Terry Beckett was one of them.

Fast forward fifty years or so, and his playing days are distant memories. But excellent memories they are, insights to a time and an age when the beautiful game was much, much different to that which has evolved into its modern version.

Terry's four granddaughters made it their grail to record as much as possible from the stories gleaned from their grandad.

****

The four young ladies sat at the living room table. Being the eldest, Hannah took charge as the discussion began to flow.

"Right, we need to be organised," she said. "It's no use throwing any old question after question at Grandad."

"Maybe we should split into pairs," said Imogen. "That would make it easier, right?"

"Good idea," remarked Trudy. "How about I partner with Phoebe, and you two join up?"

She pointed to Hannah and Imogen.

"Agreed," said Hannah. "And we'll need to set some sort of interviewing programme."

"Like what?" asked Phoebe.

"It would make sense to track Grandad's career from as early as he can remember. If he wants, he can always go back and add anything he remembers afterward."

"So, we need to do some homework first, and I know there's tons of old photographs and stuff we can use, such as old match programmes," said Imogen.

"Great," said Hannah. "I'll be coordinator for when we can visit him, and only two of us at a time, and you lot have got to be focused, especially you two."

She pointed to Phoebe and Imogen the two younger grandchildren. They giggled.

"As if," Imogen shouted.

****

"Another cuppa, Grandad?" asked Imogen. She reached across the table to take Terry's mug from him.

"Sure, love. Thanks."

Hannah made sure the plate of biscuits lay close to his right hand.

"How do you want to do this?" he asked.

"We thought it would be a good idea to sort out all these terrific old photographs and mementoes you had upstairs, and put them into a timeline," said Imogen.

"That way it makes it easier for you to remember things about them, right?" said Hannah.

Terry laughed.

"Y'know what? You girls would've made great trainers," he said. "Are we gonna hang around here all day, then? What've you got?"

Hannah and Imogen began to sort their papers and photographs into lines on the big table.

"Most of them have dates," said Imogen. "Some don't, but we can see where they match up with the ones that do have, and we can figure they were taken around the same time."

He ran his eyes along the rows and rows of documents. He stopped at one or two and peered at them before moving on to the next in line.

"Yes, these take me back, I can tell you."

"When did you first know you were good at football?" said Imogen.

"I knew it the minute I was born," said Terry, laughing. "My first four words were Mam, Dad and Manchester United."

"Cut it out, Grandad," said Hannah. "Get serious for a minute."

"I can't remember a time when we weren't outside kicking a ball around in the street and at school. In the summer holidays I used to visit my cousins in South Manchester, well Cheshire, it was posh there. They lived in Style, near Quarry Bank Mill, loads of fields to run around in. We'd play football with their pals and they'd say 'don't tell the lads that you are playing with United', and we'd hammer the opposite team. I think they were always surprised at my skill, and we'd walk away laughing," remarked Terry".

"What school did you go to?"

"Good old St. Patrick's Catholic Primary School," he said. "We had tons of kids there who were good players."

"Here's what a bunch of future world stars looked like back then," said Terry.

"Look at the goalkeeper's jersey. A big woollen thing it was, with a rollneck up to his chin. If it was raining or the ground was muddy, after a while his jersey weighed twice what it did when he put it on before the game."

The girls giggled.

St Patrick's School Team

"Any famous ones at your school?" said Imogen.

"Well, if you mean apart from me?" said Terry, with another huge smile.

"There was Nobby Stiles who went on to play for United and England. He was part of the team that won the World Cup at Wembley in 1966. Nobby is four years younger than me."

"Did you know him at school?"

"Not really, but of course when he played for United, everybody knew him. He was a fierce tackler. No holds barred on the pitch. That was in the days when players were allowed to tackle properly. None of the modern, namby-pamby protection rubbish from referees that you see nowadays. Off the field, he was the gentlest, nicest bloke you could ever meet. He wasn't very tall and wore glasses with thick black rims. You could've mistaken him for a school student. Most of the pros were like that. Bull terriers during the game. It was all about winning for your own side, but a lot of respect for the guys on the opposite team. After the match, some of the players would go for a pint or two with the same guys they'd been kicking lumps off for ninety minutes earlier in the day."

"Anyone else?" said Hannah.

"Lots of them went on from St. Patrick's to play for various teams, but another who ended up starring for United was Brian Kidd, *'Kiddo'*. He's ten years my junior."

"He won the European Cup for United, didn't he?' said Imogen.

"You've done your homework all right," said Terry. "But he didn't do it all by himself. There were some other guys in that side you might have heard of. Like Georgie Best, Bill Foulkes, and Bobby Charlton."

"Stop kidding around, Grandad. Of course, we know them, too."

"Just checking!"

"How did you go from the school football to higher levels?"

"The local scouts were always watching the school games. Every match from a certain age upward, there were guys on the sidelines. We got to know sometimes when they turned up. Other times, faces we didn't recognise would show up. That was a dead giveaway. Why else would strangers be at our matches?"

"When you knew people were there to scout, did that affect the way you played?"

"Hell, no. We were just kids. At that age, we just wanted to get on with the game and win. Winning always felt good, scoring goals was even better."

"When did it become apparent that you were a bit special?"

"I suppose it started to dawn on me when I was getting picked out of the junior team to play in a level or so higher. One day, I was put up against Wilf McGuinness. We nearly had a fight when he hit me with a full-blooded tackle, a bit unfairly. I told him, 'If you tackle me like that again, you'll be in trouble.' He said, 'I'll tackle you as I bloody well want.' I replied, 'You think you will... you're not playing with the kids in the street, y'know.' All this time, the teachers were laughing, listening to us. I wondered why they'd put me against him. When I came off the field, they said, 'You shouldn't have got so excited.' Then we went home together. You didn't hold a grudge in those days."

"Wilf became a good pal of yours, didn't he?" said Imogen.

"Aye, he did. He was what was called a wing half, nowadays he'd be an attacking midfielder. Funny how the names of positions on the field have changed. I suppose it's all the fancy coaching and strategies that's done that."

"Like what?"

"Well, the usual line up when I played was a goalie, two full backs, left and right, two wing halfs, left and right again, with a centre half, normally the biggest man in the side, and great at heading the ball. Up front, five players, right and left wingers, two inside forwards and a centre forward. Now they call the lad up front in the middle the striker, and you rarely see five guys in a forward line."

"How has that changed things, Grandad?" said Hannah.

"The art of wingers speeding to the bye-line and pinpointing crosses into the middle has almost died out."

"Were you quick?"

"Faster than a speeding bullet, love, and I still am," laughed Terry, with a wink. "I had my moments. It was part of my job to feed the crosses into people like Bobby Charlton. And by the way, that boy could really smack a ball. Here's a much later shot of him and me, sitting at the left end of the front row in the youth team at United."

The Youth Team with Terry Beckett and Bobby Charlton

"And another thing, you know, unlike today's games, there were no substitutes allowed on the field until the middle of the nineteen-sixties."

"Really? That must have made it tough," whispered Imogen pensively.

"We never thought so, because nobody was used to having subs. Not until the 1965-66 season, when the English professional league introduced the permission of one named substitute for an injured player. A year later, the named substitute could be used for any reason. It meant that the guy who was substitute was usually what we would call a utility player. Somebody who could slot in to more than one position and do a decent job of it. If a goalie got injured, an outfield player would have to put on his gloves."

"Today they name seven players as subs on the bench, and can replace three at any time, correct?" said Hannah.

"Correct," said Terry. "We only needed a minibus in those days for away matches. And the annoying thing for me to watch is when they substitute one player after another with only two or three minutes to play, even in added time at the end of a match, just to slow the game down and frustrate the opposition. It's daft. It's nothing but time wasting and almost like cheating, in my opinion."

The girls compared their notes so far, ticking off some of the questions they had put to their grandad. Without asking this time, Imogen poured more tea for all of them.

"Hang on, wait for me," she said.

She left the room and returned with another bottle of Vimto.

"Okay," said Hannah. "So far, so good. Can we go back to what happened after the St. Patrick's school football?" said Hannah.

"Hang on, hang on, wait a minute. We haven't talked yet about me playing for the Manchester Schools team. Or getting picked for the County side."

"That's what I meant. The step up from just playing for St. Pat's."

Terry sipped at his tea, blowing on it to cool the brew. He sat back in his armchair, gathering his thoughts.

"Just! St. Pats was a fabulous school."

2 ENGLISH SCHOOLS FOOTBALL

"There's a lot of old programmes here from the early fifties with your name included, Grandad," Hannah said with intrigue. "This is from a County game, Lancashire versus Cheshire, when you must have been about thirteen years old. Right?"

Terry took the pamphlet from her and went through some of the names.

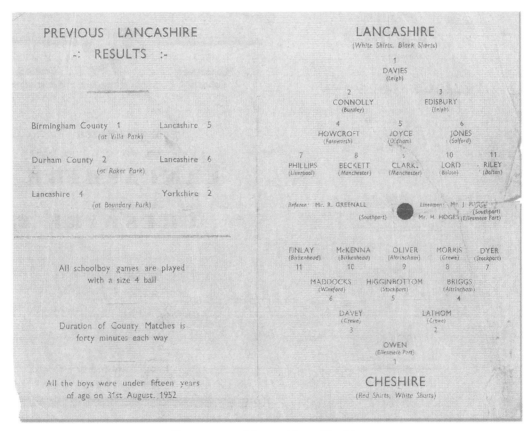

PREVIOUS LANCASHIRE
-: RESULTS :-

Birmingham County 1   Lancashire 5
(at Villa Park)

Durham County 2   Lancashire 6
(at Roker Park)

Lancashire 4   Yorkshire 2
(at Boundary Park)

All schoolboy games are played
with a size 4 ball

Duration of County Matches is
forty minutes each way

All the boys were under fifteen years
of age on 31st August, 1952

LANCASHIRE
(White Shirts, Black Shorts)

1
DAVIES
(Leigh)

2   3
CONNOLLY   EDISBURY
(Burnley)   (Leigh)

4   5   6
HOWCROFT   JOYCE   JONES
(Farnworth)   (Oldham)   (Salford)

7   8   10   11
PHILLIPS   BECKETT   CLARK.   LORD   RILEY
(Liverpool)   (Manchester)   (Manchester)   (Bolton)   (Bolton)

Referee: Mr. R. GREENALL   Linesmen: Mr. J. JUDGE
(Southport)   (Southport)
Mr. H. HODGES (Ellesmere Port)

FINLAY   McKENNA   OLIVER   MORRIS   DYER
(Birkenhead)   (Birkenhead)   (Altrincham)   (Crewe)   (Stockport)
11   10   9   8   7

MADDOCKS   HIGGINBOTTOM   BRIGGS
(Winsford)   (Stockport)   (Altrincham)
6   5   4

DAVEY   LATHOM
(Crewe)   (Crewe)
3   2

OWEN
(Ellesmere Port)
1

CHESHIRE
(Red Shirts, White Shorts)

Programme of Lancashire v Cheshire

"A lot of these lads are no longer with us, but bloomin' heck, they could play a bit of football, I can tell you. We were young boys, and they let us use a size 4 football. We only did forty minutes each half, and we would come off the pitch shattered."

"We found this one of you when you were still at school, playing for England."

Hannah handed her grandad the black and white image of a confident, fair-faced lad, arms crossed, proudly sporting the shirt with the English Schoolboys Association badge.

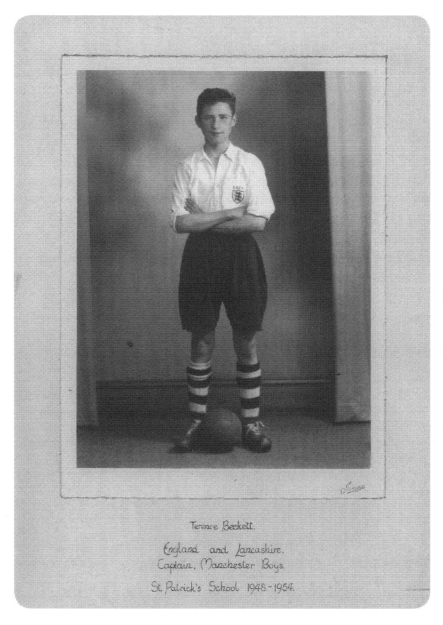

Terence Beckett.

England and Lancashire.
Captain, Manchester Boys.
St. Patrick's School 1948-1954.

Terry Beckett, England and Lancashire Captain, Manchester Boys, St Patrick's School, 1948-1954

"Yep," said Terry. "Notice the smart collar. Proper little clotheshorses, we were. They don't dress that smart these days."

"But, oh my God, look at the baggy shorts!" Imogen shrieked, pointing at the black pants.

"And don't miss the boots," said her Grandad. "Could've been built in the shipyards, and with these studs, you could climb Everest in them. The original studs were hard cork, nailed into the soles. When your boots got old and the studs wore down, sometimes the nails would push up through the bottom and give your feet hell. You knew that was time to get a new pair. God forbid you would ever think of turning up with boots that didn't shine with the dubbing polish. In fact, here's the notice from the Manchester Schools' Football Association when I was selected to play at Newton Heath Loco versus Oldham. Look what it says about the boots and stuff, '...bringing well studded boots, a change of stockings, shorts and a towel would be highly appreciated...' Do you think Ronaldo and Messi have to do that now?"

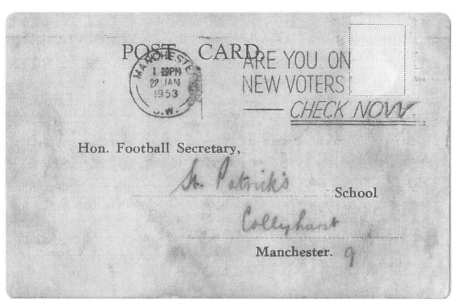

POST CARD ARE YOU ON
NEW VOTERS
— *CHECK NOW*

MANCHESTER
1 28PM
22 JAN
1953
S.W.

Hon. Football Secretary,

St. Patrick's .... School

Collyhurst

Manchester. *9*

MANCHESTER SCHOOLS' FOOTBALL ASSOCIATION.

Hon. Team Manager,
E. H. Wetton,
St. Margaret's Central School,
Whalley Range.

17, Delacourt Road,
Fallowfield,
Manchester. 14.

Date as Postmark.

CITY BOYS.

Dear Sir,   *Oldham*

    Your favour of instructing and arranging for

Beckett   to report at *Newton Heath Loco*

on *Sat. Jan 24*   bringing well studded boots, a change of
stockings, shorts and a towel would be highly appreciated.

        Yours sincerely,

at 10   *E. H. Wetton*

        Hon. Team Manager.

"I guess not," said Hannah, leading the conversation. "Hey, my Mum said you still played five-a-side at Oldham ground into your sixties. Is that true?"

"I did. And I used to run rings around them young lads during their lunch hour. It was only amateur, of course, and my game was slow, but they were often mesmerised by, what do Phoebe and Trudy call it? 'Skillin'.'"
He laughed.

"Then it would take me a week to recover."

"Oh Grandad, I remember you sat with ice and you couldn't move off the sofa when I was little. Here's a picture and a certificate, when you were selected for the English Schools Football Association versus Ireland in May, 1953."

Ireland Versus England 28 May 1953

Schools' Internationals.
The Victory Shield Competition.

This is to certify that ___T. Beckett___ was selected _Inside left_ for ___England___ -V- ___Ireland___ at ___Belfast___ on ___28th May___ ___1953___

J. McKee ___Chairman___
_C. Rice___ ___Secretary___

"And another one here," said Hannah. "You in your smart track suit, a year later, in the squad v Wales."

SCHOOLS' INTERNATIONAL MATCH

VICTORY SHIELD COMPETITION

ENGLAND 2——WALES 1

PLAYED ON THE WATFORD F.C. GROUND, 20th MARCH, 1954

Back Row: G. L. Crandon, Esq. (E.S.F.A. Council), S. W. F. Burden, Esq. (E.S.F.A. Council), E. Speight (Dagenham), F. Horne (S.E. Staffs.), J. Dean (Manchester), J. T. Hallatt (Rotherham), G. Cox (High Wycombe), A. Cooper (Reserve—Wirral), D. E. Price, Esq. (Vice-Chairman E.S.F.A.), D. Bennet (Reserve—Southampton) and H. J. Collison (Croydon).

Front Row: K. Sadler (Reserve—Chesterfield), W. R. Ward, Esq. (Secretary E.S.F.A.), J. W. Metcalfe (Crewe), A. F. Spears (Amble), G. Oliver (Altrincham), W. H. Morgan, Esq., M.B.E. (Chairman E.S.F.A.), B. Staton (Captain—Doncaster), A. J. Jeffrey (Rotherham), A. R. Rodgerson (Lambton and Hetton), R. Charlton, Esq., M.B.E. (Hon. Treasurer E.S.F.A.), and T. Beckett (Reserve—Manchester).

Team Photograph – England versus Wales, March 1954

"England won the Victory Shield 8 years running, well apart from 1965 when we let the Jocks have a chance, not bad eh?" commented Terry.

"That's a fancy-looking cap they gave you all back then," said Imogen.

"Fancy, maybe, love," said Terry. "But they were like gold to us lads."

"I still have that. Here, look. It still fits beautifully!"

"Fabulous Grandad," commented Hannah smiling.

"It is funny how memories work. It feels like yesterday when I was stood there lined up waiting to receive my cap. It felt unreal actually, being chosen to play for England. England, the finest country in the world!" Terry remarked.

"Yeah yeah, you always say that," Piped up Imogen.

"It is," replied Terry.

"That was a good time to be part of the Schools' football set up," said Terry. "Especially around Manchester. Lots of people got to know you. The administrators had you in their sights, and so did the scouts from the bigger clubs. There was a big knock-on effect when you were picked to play for the Schools Association. It led to being at the front of the queue for selection for the county and national teams as well."

"Was that how you got to sign for Manchester United?"

"It was part of it. Of course, a club like United was the aim for most of us, but the scouts played a huge role in that. They got to know where you lived, and some even just turned up at the front door to speak to your parents. My dad told me about Joe Armstrong, one of the best talent scouts that United ever had."

"What did he say about him?"

"Only good things. He was dedicated," said Terry.

He put the photographs in his hand back on the table.

"Hey, are we done yet? Can we carry this on in your next meeting?"

"Of course, Grandad," said Hannah. "We want to share the work with you, anyway. Phoebe and Trudy can follow up on this tomorrow afternoon if that's okay with you?"

"Okay. That'll let me go over some more of it, as well. And I'll see you and Imogen the meeting after that, right?"

"Sure."

Hannah got up and kissed her grandad and moved aside to let Imogen do the same.

"So, we two'll see you early next week," said Hannah. "Goodnight. Love you."

"Love you, too, hey, here you are," he said.

He gave them each a bar of chocolate.

****

The rain hadn't stopped all day. Trudy and Phoebe wiped their feet on the outside mat and stepped inside the doorway, shaking their umbrellas to take off the worst of the dripping water. They slipped off their trainers and placed them near the door in the hall. The sound of a news programme from the television in the living room greeted the girls as they pushed the door open.

"Hi, Grandad," they said in chorus.

"Hi, Trudy, Phoebe. How are you? Did you get soaked coming over?"

"Bloomin' neck, khalas!" gasped Phoebe. "We're okay. "Does it ever stop in Manchester?"

"You mean bloomin' heck? You know more Arabic than Mancunian! Aye, well you two are used to the sunshine in the Middle East, you're not used to this, are you?"

Terry pointed the remote to switch off the television and sat over in his seat at the big table. The array of cuttings and photographs were still where the cousins had left them. In the meantime, Terry had gone through them again a few times since the other girls had gone, recalling where each had been taken and the stories that every one of them held, enjoying the scenes they reproduced in his mind.

The notebooks retrieved from their bags, the pair of young ladies sat one on either side of their grandad.

"Do you want a brew, girls?" he said.

"Naa, we're fine, Nana's been filling us up with pancakes again, we're still full from breakfast," said Phoebe.

"Hannah said we could carry on talking about the scouts from the clubs," said Trudy. "You mentioned Joe Armstrong."

"You lot are thorough, you're like detectives!" said Terry. "Now, Joe, although, it must be said, he wasn't the only scout that came to watch our games. There were probably dozens of them."

"Why does his name stick with you?" asked Phoebe.

"For a start, we all knew he was scouting for United. Before him, Louis Rocca was the chief scout for the club until just after the end of the war, when Joe took his place."

"Did the scouts talk to you directly at the games?" asked Trudy.

"Not so much. It was more usual for them to have a chat with the team managers, and the school teachers who were responsible for bringing us through the levels. That's where they would find out where we all lived, our parents' names and stuff like that. Years afterward, when I became a scout myself, I followed that pattern. But let's not get ahead of ourselves. That's for later."

A compilation of badges

"When was the first time scouts came to your house?" queried Phoebe.

"I can't give you an exact date, but I must have been around fourteen or fifteen, maybe even earlier than that. Most of them were looking for boys who could step into the football academies at the clubs. I was playing a lot of games for the Manchester Schools, for Lancashire and even getting noticed at the national team levels about that time."

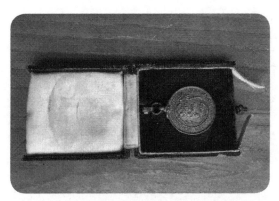

Medal from English Schools Association

"It must have felt good to have those guys trying to get you into their clubs," said Trudy.

"It was, but there was so much competition around, you really had to keep your feet on the ground. The step up to the clubs' training facilities and methods was a real eye-opener."

"Why was that?" asked Phoebe.

"The expectation levels were so high, from yourself, your parents, from the club, from your mates," said Terry. "The coaching was tough, I have to admit. No room for slackers. They wanted us to be as fit as greyhounds, and just as quick. We trained outside in all weathers. Teeming down with rain or not, made no difference. I suppose that was fair play, as you couldn't pick and choose the weather on match days. There were days in the winter when we played on snow-covered pitches. The groundsmen just shovelled the stuff away from the lines and away we went. For me, I loved it. The surface got skiddy, and as a winger, it was easier to turn the fullbacks. None of that with pitches now, with all the underground heating and all. By the way, Phoebe, I heard you won an award at your football club recently, what was it?" said Terry.

"Em, keepy-up champion for the season at Tekkers Academy, Bahrain" she said, with pride.

"Go on then, how many?"

"Seventeen, and it was against boys, too!"

"Well done. Ah, we used to play out 'til it was dark, kicking a ball against the wall and doing keepy-up. Them were the days," said Terry.

Trudy scribbled a couple of notes on her pad and lifted her head once more.

"Your parents liked Joe and he got you to sign for the Reds?" she said.

"Pretty much," said Terry, brushing cake crumbs from the front of his cardigan. "There was a lot of competition for me as well as for most of the other lads. One time, the scouts from Wolverhampton Wanderers came calling. They were a really big club in those days, with great support. Even today, they get terrific crowds through the gates at Molineux Stadium."

"What happened?" asked Phoebe.

"I was playing in one of the youth matches, and on the sidelines there was a coach from Wolves who used to be part of the set up at United. A decent guy. I didn't know it, but he had already been to see my parents and even offered them a house down in Wolverhampton, all paid for."

"Was that allowed?" asked Trudy.

"It's a long time ago, and the rules about offering inducements were a bit fudged in the fifties. Absolutely not permitted in the modern game. That's what they tell me, but I wouldn't be surprised if some arrangements still go on. The amounts of cash involved now are just silly monopoly money."

"What did he say to you?"

"He told me about my parents and the house and all that. He said if I signed with them, he would guarantee I'd be in the first team within two years. I told him he was a bit late because I'd already done the business with United. When I spoke to my dad afterward, he said he and my mum were shocked when they arrived at the front door in a big, shiny, posh car. I suppose they really were keen to get me."

"Who else came calling?" said Phoebe.

"A few clubs. One of them was Manchester City. Later, I was with them for a little while, but more of that as we go on. What else do you want to know?"

"You haven't talked about any of the games you played in, Grandad," said Trudy. "Can you tell us a bit about some of them?"

Terry leaned back and closed his eyes for a few moments, gathering his thoughts.

"Any more tea?" he asked.

"More tea, coming up," said Phoebe, reaching to take Terry's mug.

"Thanks, love. And pass me one of those chocolate biscuits, will you? This talking's hungry stuff."

He took a couple of sips and bit into the biscuit, while the girls waited patiently, ready to write the next piece.

"When they signed me up to join Manchester United Youths I was doing well as an international pick with the England Youth squad. That started a great period for me. Many of that team weren't yet fully recognised members of the first eleven. Remember, we were all young kids."

"You know one time we were going to play against Blackpool reserves. The weather was atrocious! So anyway, we are driving in snow and the next thing we are travelling up the East Lancs, a bit further on than where Hannah and Imogen live, and the driver gets out to make a call at the phone box to see if the game was still on. There were no mobiles in those days, can you imagine that? So he said the game was off and they were letting us go back to the ground and watch the first team. All the way back they were talking, saying Stanley Mathews wouldn't play today because he would be playing against Roger Burns, Captain of United and England player, and he never played against him. Stanley would be on the right wing against him, you see. Anyway, they were arguing, 'he won't play', 'he will play', I kept my mouth shut as I was the youngest in the team. When we got back we pulled up alongside the Blackpool first team coach, and we all scrambled around looking out of the window at the players getting off the coach, one said 'they'll say he has an injury and he won't play', then another said 'he's got a Crombie'. And I piped up 'what kind of injury is that'?" laughed Terry.

"Bet you don't know what a Crombie is?"

"Not a clue," remarked Trudy.

"Well it's a very expensive coat, lovely they are, and not an injury. They were all laughing at me and pulled my leg for weeks. Sir Stanley Mathews, a smart man indeed, and the only footballer for years to play professional over 35 as far as I know. He played for England over 50 times." reflected Terry.

"What did your mum and dad say when you were signed up?" said Trudy.

"They couldn't get over it. I remember my mam bought new furniture, a new suite, new beds, carpets, we had a harp too, she'd never had so much money. Y'see, I was only sixteen, and in those days, you used to give your wage to the 'house', then I got two quid a week spends. It was a lot of money. Some of my friends were working, but they had nowhere near that.

My dad was on five quid a week and I was on seventeen quid a week. The thing is, I used to just find it in my coat after practice, and knew where it had come from, of course, as they couldn't pay me that officially. I used to just find it there. My mum worked in a factory that made coats and my dad was a driver on 'the dustbins', driving all week for his five quid. I'm sure the other players were getting money in the coat pocket like me. Here's me and my dad on my wedding day. Proper gents, eh?"

Terry and his father, Samuel 'Sam'

Terry took a breath and began to list the names of some of his contemporaries.

"There was Duncan Edwards, one of the finest players ever in the English game. One of my best pals, Eddie Colman, used to be called 'Snakehips'. He had a body swerve to kill for, a bit like Ryan Giggs many years later. And a quiet lad, Bobby Charlton. What a player he turned out to be. That boy had dynamite in his boots. Later of course, along with Nobby Stiles, he was one of the magnificent team that won the World Cup for England in 1966."

"Were they all that good playing alongside you, Grandad?"

"Of course, I made them great players with the passes and crosses I served up for them," said Terry, with a deep chuckle and a twinkle in his eye.

"Stop kidding!" said Phoebe, laughing. She landed a punch on her grandad's arm.

"This was well before they became household names in the game," said Terry. "Other terrific lads in the youth team were Wilf McGuinness, Shay Brennan, Alan Rhodes, John Queenan, Dennis Fidler, Peter Jones, and Tony Hawksworth. We really enjoyed being on the same field together."

MANCHESTER UNITED YOUTH TEAM 1955
Back Row: Wilf McGuinness, John Queenan, Tony Hawksworth, Eric Jones, Alan Rhodes, Duncan Edwards.
Front Row: Bobby Charlton, Terry Beckett, Eddie Colman, K.Morgans, Shay Brennan.

"Was this the time of Matt Busby?" said Trudy.

"It was Matt Busby's foresight. He developed and coached us."

"Did he call you the 'Busby Babes' then?"

"No. The man who did that first was a sports writer for the Manchester Evening News, Frank Nicklin. He wrote it when Matt gave twenty-two-year old Roger Byrne and eighteen-year-old Jackie Blanchflower their first games, against Liverpool on November 24th, 1951. Apparently, Matt didn't think much of the term, and preferred 'Red Devils'. However, since then, given everything that happened later, there's so much attached to the name."

"It really was such a big change having so many young players in the side, wasn't it?" said Trudy.

"Many years later, the great Alex Ferguson did something similar with his young team," said Terry. "In August 1995, Match of the Day pundit, Alan Hansen, foolishly criticised Alex with a comment that haunts him to this day, and has gone down in football folklore, especially at Old Trafford, when he said, 'You can't win anything with kids.' Alex's youngsters won the title."

"What was your first game for the club?" asked Phoebe, pencilling her list of questions.

"After I signed with United, my first game with them was on December 11th, 1954. A date I will never forget. I was all of 16 years, 1 month and 24 days old."

"How was the game?" said Phoebe.

"To be honest, I can't remember anything much about it, or even who we were playing against. I was just thrilled to be wearing a Manchester United jersey. I think we won. It was the start of lots of playing time in United's Youth, A, and Reserves teams."

"You're bound to say you always won," said Trudy.

Her grandad laughed.

"We did!" he said giving her a grimace of mock surprise. "We were United! We were the best in the world! At least, that's what our coaches told us. And y'know something? We started to believe that."

"That's psychology, isn't it?" enquired Trudy.

"Big word, that, Trudy, but you're right," said Terry. "If you don't believe you can win and be the best, there's half the battle gone right there and then. If you look at our record, it speaks for itself. There was a Youth Cup competition, where we were so formidable, we looked almost unbeatable. United won it for the first five years of its existence. It was a real honour to reach that stage. My whole universe was football. I lived, ate and breathed it. Most of us were just the same. Getting selected to join the Busby Babes was special and everybody felt that. People would stop us to say hello in the street. It was a bit embarrassing sometimes, to be honest, and funnily enough, also a wee bit of a nuisance. I can well understand why the modern superstars find it a bit much when the fans go nuts when they're around.

It's part of the price they pay for being at that level. Without the fans, the players are nothing. I was only young, yet I used to have all my suits tailor-made by a pretty famous local man, I think his name was Walter Peers. I worked on rewiring his house years later and he said 'try that overcoat on.' It was lovely, and he told me to take it, but I didn't."

"Tell us a bit about the Youth Cup games," said Phoebe.

Terry puffed out his cheeks and rubbed the sides of his forehead with his fingers, trying to recall the details.

"Why don't you ask Hannah and Imogen to carry on with this in the next get together, and give me time to make some proper sense of it for you all? We can talk about Jimmy Murphy and what he did with the Youth team. I think you'll find that interesting."

"It's all interesting, Grandad. Right. We'll tell them what we've covered until now, and they can carry on with the rest."

"It looks as if the rain's back on," said Terry. "Put your hoods up now and make sure your sneakers don't leak."

Both girls giggled.

"See you soon," said Trudy. "Bye. Love you."

"Love you too. Bye."

As the door closed behind his granddaughters, Terry smiled to himself. So many things he'd forgotten over the years. He was enjoying these trips down memory lane.

3 MANCHESTER UNITED YOUTH TEAM

The Saturday morning visit from Hannah and Imogen began early. With no school to distract the girls, it also meant they could spend a bit more time with Terry.

"Bloomin' heck, it's the crack of dawn! How are you matching up your notes with Trudy and Phoebe?" he asked.

"Easy," said Hannah. "We write out our notes on our laptops when we go home, and share them with each other. That way, we can track the flow of your stories, and not bother you with duplication of things."

"Ingenious," said Terry. "How about the pictures and photographs?"

"We do the same with them, Grandad,' said Imogen.

"Proper little editors, aren't you?" he said. "I was asking you that because when Trudy and Phoebe were here a couple of days ago, they wanted to get some material about the United Youth team and said you would carry on with that today."

"And that's what we'll be doing," said Hannah. "We know everything we ask each other. Good isn't it!"

Terry held his hands up in mock surrender.

"No argument here," he said. "I've done a bit of homework and thinking for today's session."

The notebooks were open and ready on the table.

"I thought I'd give you some background for the couple of years before I got into the side."

"Excellent," exclaimed Imogen. "Like proper research, you mean."

"Like proper research, as you say. All the clubs had junior squads and youth teams anyway. They belonged to various leagues around the city, and up and down the country. How else were they gonna get practice? After the Second World War, the country was still in rationing mode, although that was nearly finished by the early fifties. The emergence of the FA's Youth Cup Tournament took quite a while to get up and running. In the months after the war finished in 1945, the idea was seeded with the English FA to run a youth tournament to include all the county football associations throughout England, but took several years to really get going."

"Why was that?" asked Hannah.

"I'm not sure exactly what the problem was, but it seems the clubs themselves didn't instantly share the FA's view about how good it would be in revitalising the game for younger players who hadn't yet reached a senior enough level to get into full professional football. The clubs had no objection to the FA arranging and organising regular youth team internationals, and so these went ahead okay."

"And you got selected in some of these, didn't you?' said Imogen.

"Yes, I did. It was a great way for young, up and coming players to get noticed by the big clubs and the scouts. Eventually, Sir Joe Richards, former president of the English Football League, pushed the idea to formulate the FA Youth Cup. It probably wasn't recognised at the time for what it was - a terrific step forward for the development of the game in England. You hear a lot of talk today about getting back to the grass roots level of football in England. This was really where it all began. Joe's plan didn't impress the league clubs themselves so much, but the FA jumped at it and quickly got it live. The FA Youth Cup was born."

"What year was that?" asked Imogen.

"It started in the 1952-1953 season, when Manchester United started as Division One champions. Matt Busby had United zinging the previous season, with fifty-seven points, beating Tottenham Hotspur into second place by a margin of four points. How about that for pressure on the youth team to perform!"

"Did they?" said Hannah.

"In bucketloads, my love. In bucketloads. The youth team monopolised the FA Youth Cup, as I've said before, winning it in the first five years, straight. Many of the youth team from that era went on to become legends, not only at United, but also internationally acknowledged as among the best the world had seen."

"What made them so unbeatable?" said Imogen.

"The whole approach to building on the youngsters as the future of the club began with Sir Matt Busby. To be precise, he was just plain 'Matt Busby' until he got his knighthood in 1968. I'll tell you more about him later. He had good people supporting him. Jimmy Murphy was responsible for training and looking after us lads. He did a smashing job. The year before I was in the side, the 1953/54 season, he introduced several new faces, who strengthened the team massively."

"Do you remember the names, Grandad?" asked Imogen.

"Hard to forget them, love. Jimmy brought in a goalie, eighteen-year-old Tony Hawksworth, from Sheffield. Later, he represented his country at schoolboy and youth levels. In defence, he added guys like Alan Rhodes and Ivan Beswick. There was Bobby Harrop, from Margate, who played centre half. He could also fill the midfield positions. Don't leave out my mate, Wilf McGuinness, Manchester born, and a committed Red through and through. When he joined the club as a wing half in 1953, he was only fifteen. Not many would have foreseen how well, and for how long, he would go on to serve the club with such fierce passion. In a different era, Roy Keane's style and tenacity reminded me of him a lot. At the same time, another fifteen-year-old boy came aboard, who would become a household name within a few years. Bobby Charlton."

"So, you saw Bobby and these players when they were just boys, really?" said Imogen.

"They were only boys, but fitter and stronger than a lot of men around them. I mentioned Joe Armstrong before. After the war, he took the place of Louis Rocca as Manchester United's head scout. Joe was responsible for bringing in Duncan Edwards and Bobby, two of the best finds anywhere in football of that period or any other. The young Charlton was playing in the east Northumberland Schools football team when Joe first saw him. About a year later, he already had him signed up for Old Trafford. Duncan was still in the United youth team at that time, showing week after week why he was considered among the best, if not the best player of his generation."

"Awesome," said Imogen.

"Aye, it was a special time, with a special set of lads," said Terry. "That season, they met Wolverhampton Wanderers again in the final. Wolves had a good team, and they were keen to get their own back for the defeat in the final the previous year. The first leg was at Old Trafford at the end of May, and a real ding-dong match it was. There was a crowd of more than 18,000. Not bad for a youth match, eh? The score swung back and forth, great stuff for a neutral supporter, although I doubt if there were many neutrals in the stadium that day. Big Duncan notched the first for us, then Joe Bonson hit back to level it. Joe was an excellent striker. That lad could hit goals for whoever he played for. After he left Wolves, he had spells with Cardiff City, Doncaster Rovers and Scunthorpe, among others. Then Jimmy Murray, another lad who knew his way to goal, put Wolves ahead. He bagged more than two hundred goals for Wolves in eight seasons, not a bad haul in any league. He later joined Manchester City. Things were looking tough for United when Bobby Mason got a third for the away side. But in football, as you know, nothing's ever done until the final whistle goes. David Pegg, a young outside left from Doncaster, had taken over the mantle of team captain from Ron Cope for this final. In the true to form character of a real captain, he had a great impact on the game. He scored from the penalty spot to haul the deficit back to just one goal. And who else but Edwards to bang in the equalizer? The drama still wasn't over. Wolves hit another one from John Fallon, nudging ahead 4 - 3. They must have thought it was done and dusted. Not so. David Pegg hammered in his second of the match and it finished up all square at 4 – 4."

"They all must have been exhausted at the end," said Hannah.

"I think a lot of adrenalin would've had most of them tanked up," said Terry. "They only had to wait for three days to get the second leg under way at Wolves. It was another very tight match, but only one goal in it this time around. Team captain, David Pegg, led from the front again and scored the winner to make sure United held onto the Cup with an overall aggregate of 5 – 4. United's Youth squad were riding high."

"You joined them the next season," said Hannah. "It must have been a hard act to follow."

"Competition for places is always good, love. The spirit was terrific. Even if you didn't play one week, but did so the next, you were still part of the team. It takes a whole season or a whole competition to win something in the end."

"That's like when we do group things in class at school, Grandad," said Imogen. "We all help each other."

"A hundred percent like that," said Terry. "Now, let's have another brew."

"Here you go," said Hannah, handing the refilled mug across. "The next year was when you got into the team. Can you tell us a bit about that?"

"Just try and stop me, love! One time, when I was only sixteen and we were in London, playing Tottenham on the Thursday, then on the Saturday, I couldn't believe it, we were all in front row seats at the London Palladium. It was the first time I'd seen Nat King Cole. He was phenomenal."

Terry stood up and announced with a flourish of his hand and a majestic bow, like a Master of Ceremonies, "A night." He paused for effect. "At the London Palladium!"

The girls laughed out loud.

"Here's the glamour snapshot of the team for the final," said Terry. "What a set of posers, eh? David Beckham, eat your heart out. Talking of which, your Mum, Clare, sat next to, what did they call her, 'Posh Spice'? That was years later, at a match once at Old Trafford, before they were married. Now, there's a few changes in this team photo from the previous year. There's me, of course, second from the left at the back row. The handsome fella with the flyaway collar!"

1954 – 1955

"Grandad, behave yourself," said Imogen.

"And my Mum and Dad are in the stand behind watching, see you can see them there," said Terry.

He pointed to the picture and was quiet for a few seconds.

"We had Peter Jones turning out for us for the first time. He was a local lad, and a good defender. Another really solid lad, also locally born, and who later became a regular first team player was Shay Brennan."

Terry pointed out the new faces.

"In that 1954/55 run up, we were drawn against Chelsea in the semi-final," he continued. "Their manager, the famous Chelsea ex-player, Ted Drake, had also put together a useful team of youngsters, so the rivalry was good. In the first leg at Stamford Bridge on April 16th, 1955, the result was 2 - 1 in our favour. Duncan Edwards got both our goals. Back at Old Trafford, the second leg drew 30,000 spectators on a Saturday morning. That shows you how keen the fans were. We went behind 2 - 1 by half time and Edwards moved up to centre forward. It must have caused their centre half a wobble or two. He was truly the all-round player. Shortly after the whistle for the second half, I floated in a peach of a cross. Big Duncan rose above everybody, like a dolphin soaring out of the water and hammered it home with his head to get us level and put us through to the final."

"What did that feel like, getting to play in a cup final in your first year with the team?" said Imogen.

"It was great, love. Not only the final, but the whole season's programme. We were made to feel as if we were special, and on balance, I really think we were. The toughest match we had that season, I remember, was against Barnsley, before we faced Chelsea. Once we overcame them, I felt we were on a good roll, and truly we'd go on and win the cup."

"Who did you play in the final?" asked Imogen.

1954–55: Manchester United vs. West Bromwich Albion
(4-1 and 3-0, 7-1 aggregate)

First Leg
Old Trafford, 27 April 1955
Manchester United – West Bromwich Albion 4–1 (2–0)
1–0 40 min. Bobby Charlton
2–0 43 min. Eddie Colman
3–0 67 min. Eddie Colman
3–1 68 min. Barry Hughes
4–1 85 min. Duncan Edwards
Attendance: 16,696

Manchester United			West Bromwich Albion		
No.	**Position**	**Player**	**No.**	**Position**	**Player**
1 ✚ GK		Tony Hawksworth	1 ✚ GK		Mick Cashmore
2 ✚ DF		John Queenan	2 ✚ DF		Ray Whale
3 ✚ DF		Alan Rhodes	3 ✚ DF		John Rogers
4 ✚ MF		Eddie Colman (c)	4 ✚ MF		Chuck Drury
5 ✚ MF		Peter Jones	5 ▬ MF		Barry Hughes
6 ✚ MF		Wilf McGuinness	6 ✚ MF		Barry Cooke
7 ✚ FW		Terry Beckett	7 ✚ FW		Dick Maynes
8 ▬ FW		Shay Brennan	8 ✚ FW		Maurice Setters
9 ✚ FW		Duncan Edwards	9 ✚ FW		Dick McCartney
10 ✚ FW		Bobby Charlton	10 ✚ FW		Alec Jackson
11 ✚ FW		Dennis Fidler	11 ✚ FW		Graham Williams
			Manager ✚		Unknown
Manager ▬		Jimmy Murphy			

"The Baggies, West Bromwich Albion. To be honest, the first leg at Old Trafford caused us very little trouble. We won it 4 – 1, with goals from Bobby Charlton and Duncan, as usual. Our skipper, Eddie Colman, added a couple more. Barry Hughes got their consolation goal. In the second leg over at their place, The Hawthorns, we piled on the agony, winning 3 – 0. With a three-goal advantage from the first leg, they would have to score four, and we knew we weren't gonna lose it. I managed to net the first one. I belted down the wing and smacked the ball as hard as I could across the keeper from an acute angle. It just flew past him into the net and we were one up. That kinda finished it right there and then. It took the guts out of the Baggies. Eddie Colman got the other two in the last two minutes. Bang, bang, and that was that. Manchester United remained unbeaten in the Youth Cup, with three successful finals on the trot."

Terry waited while the girls finished their notes.

"Here's a bit of trivia for you both," he said. "In the team line-ups for each of the Youth Cup finals in 1954 and 1955, all the players who took part were Englishmen apart from only two, one from each club. Shay Brennan, who's Irish, and Barry Hughes, a Welshman. Changed days, indeed."

Hannah closed her notebook.

"That's a lot of stuff covered today, Grandad," she said. "Trudy and Phoebe'll be here tomorrow in the afternoon. We'll get back and type up this lot. So far so good."

"Okay, sounds good, love. And I'll expect you again sometime early next week, right?"

"Right," said Imogen, giving Terry a big hug. "See you then."

4 MUNICH

For their Sunday session, Trudy and Phoebe took up the same seats as before, one on each side of Terry.

"Tell me something, just out of interest," he said.

"What?" the pair asked together.

"When Hannah and Imogen come here, they both sit opposite me. Why do you go either side?"

Phoebe stood up with her arms akimbo, wearing a serious look on her face.

"I thought that would be obvious, Grandad," she said.

"Beats me. Why?"

"So that you can't run away, silly!"

The girls shrieked with laughter, while Terry grinned back at them.

"Ah, you're too quick for me, girls," he said. "Where do we start today?"

"You've shared with us up until the Cup Final with the youth team at the end of April 1955," said Trudy. "Do you want to carry on from there?"

Terry rubbed his chin and leaned back in his chair, with his hands locked behind his neck.

"The next couple of years were a mixture of great fun, a lot of hard work, and toward the end of it, a bit disappointing," he began. "I told you before, we were all considered part of the family, training together, having a laugh as mates and so on. We swam in the canals in Manchester like all the other neighbourhood lads. In the off season, in the summertime, we always got involved in street games and in the local park away from the club. Kickabouts with our other mates. Nobody thought themselves too high and mighty. The club never knew about these games. They'd have given us hell. We weren't supposed to do that as we could easily have gotten injured, but we still did it, anyway. You're only young once. Eddie Colman was my best buddy during that time."

"You were playing with him a lot at United?" said Trudy.

"Yes, but I wasn't getting as many games in the A team as I would've liked. I thought, rightly or wrongly, that Jimmy Murphy wasn't giving me a fair chance, with the result I wasn't getting picked for enough games in my view."

"What happened?" said Trudy.

"One of the scouts for Manchester City had a drink with my dad in the 'Lion and Lamb' pub in Blackley one night. That led to me signing for City in November 1957. In the end, it probably wasn't the best decision to make, but y'know, being young and ambitious, we all wanted to get into the higher levels as soon as we could."

"Didn't you enjoy it?" asked Phoebe.

"Not really. I played in the City B team for a few weeks. It didn't have the same feel as with United. I had lots of mates at Old Trafford, although I did know some of the City lads, too. The atmosphere was different. It didn't take long for me to reverse the decision and go back to Old Trafford. Not long after that the Munich air crash happened."

"I've read a lot about that, Grandad," said Trudy.

"I haven't," said Phoebe. "Do you feel like talking about it? It's a bit strange, eh?"

Terry smiled and reached out to touch Phoebe's hand and squeeze it gently.

"Y'know, for your age, you're very sensitive, love," he said. "For a long time after the crash, I couldn't and wouldn't talk about it. But time's a marvellous healer. Of course, I'll tell you about it, and about the lads who didn't come back."

"Only if you're okay with it, Grandad," said Trudy.

"I'm fine. Of course, the day it all happened, everybody was initially stunned with shock and disbelief."

****

64

Terry sat back and took a few breaths, the memories from sixty years before came swirling back again, as they had done in his head hundreds of times since the tragedy.

Belonging to a team of any kind brings special relationships. The Busby Babes were not just any team. This group was unique. Nowhere in the history of the English game had such a collection of skills like theirs been brought together. The older, seasoned professionals in the squad, such as Roger Byrne, Ray Wood and Johnny Berry, mingled with the young bloods, Charlton, Duncan and Colman, and had ignited the imagination of the fans and the press. The future of Manchester United was clearly mapped for success. The face of the game was being changed. The excitement and expectation week after week, month on month, had a pace all of its own. The prospect of establishing something very special was palpable.

The tragedy in Munich came as a hammer blow to these hopes.

Grief is a multi-layered emotion. At a personal level, it expresses itself in the most intense way. In a group, it serves as a bonding, bringing people together in a common cause. As a national outpouring, it transcends everyday life.

Such was the result of the Munich air crash.

The impact on Terry Beckett was deeper than merely one man's feelings for anonymous individuals who perished. Among those who died were personal friends. Men, barely out of their teens, who had played and worked together on the coaching fields and football pitches up and down the country. These were Terry's mates, his buddies, as close a brotherhood imaginable. Only a handful of others were privy to that band, part of the indefinable camaraderie of shared experiences.

The insights from Terry on the individual team mates are unique and precious, as they record first hand his opinions on the array of precocious playing talent at Old Trafford in the late 1950s.

****

"Let me give you the background first," said Terry. "You might have heard it before, but here's what happened."

He laced his fingers and leaned forward with his chin on his hands.

"United had completed the return leg of their quarter final tie against Belgrade Red Star in Yugoslavia, now renamed Serbia. They drew 3 – 3, to take the aggregate score over two legs to 5 – 4 to progress to the semi-finals. The route on the way home to England meant a transit stopover in Munich. The weather was dreadful. Snow, ice, you name it. The worst of a European winter in Germany. The record tells us the co-pilot was at the controls for the take off. At exactly 14:19, the Munich control tower gave the all-clear signal for take-off. When the plane was moving down the runway, the pilot noticed a fluctuating pressure gauge and the engines didn't sound quite right, so that take-off was abandoned. A wee while after that, a second attempt to get off was also abandoned because the engines were over-accelerating. All the passengers were disembarked to the airport lounge to wait for further information and instructions. In the meantime, the snow started again, a very heavy snowfall."

"Why didn't they just wait until it all cleared up?" said Trudy.

"God knows, love," said her grandad. "Most of the passengers believed they wouldn't be flying anytime soon. Duncan Edwards sent a telegram to his landlady telling her that all the flights out of the airport were cancelled and he wouldn't be back until the next day. Poor lad, he and many others never came back at all."

"But they did try again and the crash happened, right?" said Phoebe.

"Aye, they did. Apparently, the captain was keen to get them back to Manchester that evening. He was an experienced lad, and he called the shots. The station engineer had suggested holding the plane overnight to get the thing retuned, but the captain felt the runway was long enough to get her off the ground safely. Everybody was called back after fifteen minutes."

Terry leaned back in his chair, his lips drawn tight. He stared at the table, his gaze fixed on the rows of photographs. His eyes began to moisten. After all these years, the tragedy in Munich still provoked great sadness.

"Are you alright with this, Grandad?" said Phoebe, touching his sleeve gently. "We don't have to carry on right now."

"It's okay, love," said Terry, quietly. "Y'see, there's something I don't think you know."

"What's that?" asked Trudy.

"On the day the group flew out from Manchester for the European tie, I was sick in bed, not something usual for me, fit as a fiddle, normally. I got my mam, your Grandma, to call in to the club and tell Matt Busby I had a severe dose of the 'flu and couldn't play."

"Otherwise, you would have been on that plane, Grandad?" said Phoebe, her eyes open wide.

"Exactly," said Terry. "There but for the grace of God. A few days later, when I had recovered and was up and about again, I was getting off the train in Piccadilly when I saw the newspaper headline about the crash. My blood ran cold. It was the worst day of my life. Horrific. All my pals that I used to run around with were gone. Just like that. It was too much to take in, how many of my close buddies had died. When I went to Eddie Colman's funeral, I remembered he and I always used to sit together, everywhere we travelled. It's strange to think about it, even now. Several times since, I went to his house, and his dog was always sitting at the door, waiting for Eddie to come home. He wasn't to know his master came back in a coffin."

He sighed.

"However, it wasn't my time then. Unfortunately, it was theirs. When the plane took off for the final time, some of the boys had moved to the rear of the cabin, thinking it would be safer there if anything went wrong. The take-off run speed reached nearly 120 knots. That was the level above which it wasn't safe to abort the flight, but the pilot realised they weren't gonna make it, as their speed began to drop. The plane skidded from the runway and crashed into a fence. The left wing detached, hitting a house, setting it on fire. The main fuselage smacked into a wooden hut which held a truck laden with fuel and tyres. You can imagine the hellish result."

The girls said nothing. They knew that their grandad was replaying the scene in his head as he probably had done hundreds of times since February 6th, 1958.

"I think we'll stop now, Grandad," said Trudy assertively. "Hannah and Imogen can carry on next time."

Terry didn't argue with her.

"Okay," he said. "Tell them I'll talk about the lads in the next meeting."

5 THE REDS WHO NEVER CAME BACK

The photos were mostly black and white and still scattered across the cloth on the table, but Terry had rearranged some of them. The plate of biscuits hadn't been touched yet.

Imogen was busy bringing the teapot from the kitchen.

"Right, Hannah, I've done my bit," she remarked. "You can pour. Remember what Grandad said about teamwork!"

Terry laughed out loud.

"A proper little taskmaster, isn't she?" he said to Hannah. "It would be hard work training under her eye."

"Yep," said Hannah, giggling.

She noticed the semi-circle of photographs in front of Terry.

"Are these the players from the crash?" she asked.

"They are exactly that, my love. It'll make it easier for you and me to use these to tell you a bit about each of them, as I knew them. I've sorted them, first of all into the lads who didn't make it home, and after that, I'll talk about the survivors. I thought it would be good to say what I knew about each of them, and to describe what happened to each of them who came back alive following Munich. I've been thinking a lot about them since Trudy and Phoebe's meeting at the weekend."

"That's great," said Imogen.

Terry reached out and picked up the nearest photograph.

"This is my best mate, Eddie Colman. He was born not far from Old Trafford, in Archie Street in Salford. You could say he was destined to step into the club from that short distance away. He was on the short side, only about five feet seven, but he had football magic in his veins. He played wing half. The club got him straight from school into the youth team in 1952. Three years later, he was holding his position in the first team. When he had the ball at his feet, it was impossible to get it away from him. He had this body swerve that was so good his nickname was 'Snakehips'. He once played against Len Shackleton, one of the league's best players. We asked him how he got on against him, and he joked it was easy. He was always one for a laugh. At times, I've seen as many as three players around Eddie trying to stop him, and none got even close. Think of Paul Scholes, and you'll get some idea what he was like. He shared Scholesie's awareness of where other teammates were on the pitch."

"He was that good?" said Imogen.

"He really was. I looked up the records for his time with the club. I've done the same for the other players, so that I can give you details as we go through each of them. Eddie made 108 appearances for the first team, and collected two First Division winners' medals and one runners-up medal in the FA Cup when they lost to Aston Villa 2 – 1 in the final. Sadly, he was the youngest person on the plane to die that day. The University of Salford has a hall of residence named in his honour, the Eddie Colman Court. There was also a statue of him at his graveside in Weaste Cemetery in Salford, but some crazy vandals badly damaged it. When it was repaired it was moved to his father's home. Both his parents, Dick and Elizabeth have since passed away and are buried alongside their son."

Terry placed the photograph back on the table.

"He was a great buddy. Eddie and I would often go to the dancing at the Ritz in Manchester and the Sale Locarno. They had one of these great sprung, wooden dance floors and we'd hang around near the stage there. He was set to get married. We used to get invited to the front of the queues and walk past the long line because the doormen knew us."

Terry shuffled the photographs and picked up another one.

"Here's Roger Byrne. Another Manchester-born boy, he was raised in the Gorton district of the city. Joe Armstrong is credited with bringing Roger to the club as an amateur in 1949, and soon afterward he signed on as a professional. He's reckoned as the first of the Busby Babes. The club made him captain in the 1955-56 season and he remained in that role until his death. There have been other full back defenders with more style and panache, but Roger had other special qualities that made him a standout leader. In the fifties, full backs were generally expected to stay back, nearer their goalie than the halfway line. He would have none of that. It wasn't unusual to see him marauding forward, pressing up the backs of his own left wing-half and left winger. But forget that. His greatest asset was the ability to inspire and motivate others on the pitch. As players, of course, we all had self-motivation, but the driving force behind every great team is somebody who can pick you up when your head drops a bit. Somebody who shows you by sheer guts and example what it means to wear the Reds' shirt. I talked earlier about the similarity between Eddie Colman and Paul Scholes. For Roger, think of Roy Keane. No nonsense. No compromise. We are Manchester United! We are winners!"

"Wow!" said Hannah. "He sounds a bit special."

"There were so many special guys in the team and at the club back then, love," said Terry. "Much of that was developed by the mentality of the coaches and the managers, but I'll talk about these later. Roger picked up league winners' medals three times. In 1952, 1956 and 1957, and was also a runner up in the FA Cup Final against Aston Villa."

"He also played for England, didn't he?" Imogen enquired.

"My, you girls are hot with your homework, I must say," said their grandad.

"You're correct, yet again. The national side manager, Walter Winterbottom gave him his first cap for his country against the old enemy, Scotland, in 1954, and he turned out for 33 consecutive matches in a row for England starting then, a record for consecutive games by any player."

Terry shook his head slowly.

"Added to the sadness of his passing away in Munich, was that he left behind his wife, Joy, who was expecting their first baby, having been married the previous year. His son, Roger Junior, was born six months later. He became a ball boy at Old Trafford in the late sixties and early seventies, which is a nice continuation of the family's connection with the club. Like many of the others, Roger Senior has a street named after him, the Roger Byrne Close, in a new housing development near the city centre. Our captain was the oldest player killed in the crash."

The next photograph showed a young man, arms folded, exuding an air of confidence.

"Who's he?" said Imogen.

"That's Duncan Edwards," said Hannah to her sister. "I've seen pictures of him before."

"That is indeed young Duncan," confirmed her grandad. "There can't be too many people who can say they played in the same side as him, but I did, several times. Y'know, a lot of nonsense gets talked about a certain player being great, or another footballer being the best ever, but Duncan really was very, very special. He was the complete package. For his age, there was nobody comparable. Big, strong, of course, but he was more than that.

He oozed skill and presence on any pitch. Quicker than most, he could hit with either foot, and scored some unstoppable goals. I mentioned earlier, he banged one in with his head against Chelsea, from one of my crosses in the Youth Cup. He was a standout even at the age of twelve, when United scout, Jack O'Brien saw him playing in a school match in Dudley. He told Matt Busby about him, and it came as no surprise when he signed for the club. He made his debut for United when he was only sixteen, the youngest player ever to play in the English First Division, and went on to appear in over 150 senior matches. He point-blank refused to listen to offers to join other clubs. He also became the youngest player since the war to play for his country, and turned out 18 times for them at the highest level."

"A bit like Wayne Rooney, Grandad?" said Hannah.

"Yes, there's some similarities, although maybe I'm biased, having played with Duncan, I'd say he edged it over Rooney. But for sure, the same kind of impact with fans and the press was there for Duncan. If you look at his professional career record, which was only five years, he was in the side that won two Football League titles for United, as well as two FA Charity Shields, and they also got to the European Cup semi-finals. There was a bit of a spat between United and Wolves over Duncan, when the Wolves manager, Stan Cullis accused United of improperly offering financial inducements to his family, all of which Matt Busby denied fiercely. Anyway, Duncan said he'd always had a preference for joining Manchester, and that was that. Pass me another brew, love."

Imogen took Terry's mug to top it up, but only a trickle came from the pot.

"I'll get another one going," she said, heading for the kitchen. "Wait for me."

A few minutes later, they settled in again, pencils at the ready.

"Duncan was a phenomenally strong young man," said Terry. "His body took a heck of a battering in the crash. He had severe injuries, so much so, even if had survived, the doctors were doubtful he would ever be able to play football again. Despite superhuman efforts to keep him going with an artificial kidney, his blood refused to clot properly. It was a losing battle, but one he fought bravely. He died two weeks after the crash."

"That's terrible," said Imogen. "And terrible for all of them."

"Aye, love, it was," said Terry. "Bobby Charlton said Duncan was so good, he was the only player that made him feel inferior. Tommy Docherty, who was United's manager in the seventies, knew a thing or two about football. He said Duncan would have gone on to be known as the best player the world had ever seen, with his all-round natural ability. Some praise, that."

"There are so many photos left there, Grandad," said Hannah, gesturing at the table.

It was strange to see such an array of young faces, the starkness of the black and white photography highlighting them better than any colour images could, witness to the distance of years since their lives were dramatically impacted sixty years in the past.

Terry stood up, pressing his lower back with his hands and stretching his shoulders backward. He moved his head slowly from side to side in an exaggerated way, ridding himself of the stress that telling the memories was causing.

"Are you okay, Grandad?" asked Imogen again.

"No worries, love," he said. "Let's get on with it."

"Hey, listen to this story about being a born leader. So we were taken to a golf club for a steak dinner, that was a real treat you know then, and we thought the steak was tough as none of us cold cut it, a place like that and the steak was tough, it didn't add up. Anyway, Duncan stood up, walked into the kitchen and came back with a load of steak knives. You see, he had initiative on and off the pitch," shared Terry.

Still standing, he picked up the next photograph and sat down, turning the picture toward his granddaughters.

"I've told you about this lad, David Pegg. Kinda quiet off the field, but he let his skill do the talking on it. He played as a left winger for the club and once for England. Some say he was about to break through big time internationally, but Munich happened. He took after his father, who was a talented amateur player. I suppose it was in the genes, eh? He's another one who picked up a couple of league title medals and got United into two European Cup semi-finals. He signed for the club when he was fifteen, straight from school, and got his first outing with the senior side when he was only seventeen. United really were never scared of putting youngsters into the side in those days. A bit of 'if they're good enough, they're old enough', I think. No surprise really, then, when the Busby Babes began to appear. When his parents eventually passed away, they were buried next to him in the Redhouse Cemetery."

"He was the one you told us about being captain in the Youth Cup, right?" said Hannah.

"Yes, he was the star performer against Wolves in the 1954 final," said Terry.

"This one's Tommy Taylor. Another terrific goal scorer."

"What a lovely smile in that photograph," said Imogen. "He's handsome."

"Lovely smile maybe, but Tommy terrified defences everywhere he played," said Terry. "When he was just sixteen, scouts signed him up from the local colliery team to join Barnsley. That was in 1949. A year later, he made his first team debut for them in October. His second game in the senior side was spectacular. He notched a hat-trick against Queens Park Rangers in a 7 - 0 scoreline. There was no stopping him after that. He banged in 26 goals in only 44 matches for Barnsley. Along came United and bought him for £29,999."

"That's a strange amount,' said Hannah. "Why not £30,000?"

"Simple," said Terry. "Matt Busby was very clever. He didn't want Tommy to be burdened as being a £30,000 player. A nice touch from Matt was during the negotiations, he took a £1 note from his wallet and gave it to the tea lady who'd been serving them all the while the discussions were going on. Matt had real class, y'know. By the way, compare that fee to today's monopoly money transfer fees of £30,000,000 and more. Daft prices, if y'ask me. And that's for what sometimes look like only average players. I wonder how much your old Grandad would be worth in today's market, eh?"

Imogen shrieked.

"You're priceless, Grandad!" she said. "You know that!"

She came over to Terry and threw her arms around him.

"Okay," said Terry. "Call Old Trafford now and tell them you want to sell me to them for hundreds of millions!"

"I'll do it later," said Imogen. "Tell us more about Tommy Taylor."

"Well, that £29,999 transfer fee was against the background of so many other clubs looking to sign him. Wolves, Derby County and Sheffield Wednesday among them. It made him one of the most expensive signings to date in the English game. He delivered for the money. He got two goals in his first game for United, and went on to be a part of the team that won two league titles and lost in the Cup Final to Aston Villa. He scored in the final. In 1957, Matt Busby turned down a bid for him from the Italian giants, Internazionale, for £65,000, which would have been a world transfer record. He played 19 times for his country and netted 16 goals, not a bad tally, twice getting hat-tricks.

Tommy was a prolific scorer at centre forward, and marvellous with headers. The old-style target man. He got 112 goals for United in 166 league matches. He had just turned 26 when he died in Munich, and was engaged to be married. He's buried in his hometown at Monk Bretton Cemetery, Barnsley."

"We found something in our research about where some of the players lived," said Hannah. "There's a blue plaque on the wall at number 22, Greatstone Road in Stretford. Manchester United used the boarding house there as lodgings for their single players, didn't they?"

"Aye. You're right, love. Tommy lived there, as well as David Pegg, and for a wee while, Mark Jones. They all died in the plane crash. That plaque was sponsored by the Stretford High School, about fifty yards away from where they lived. It was a local history project by the pupils of the school, and it was unveiled by the famous cricket umpire, Dickie Bird. Dickie went to school with Tommy in Barnsley. I used to live in Oldham Road and caught the 65 bus to get to Old Trafford. Tommy got on a few stops before we reached the ground, and then we'd walk down together. We met a lad with a bike and Tommy asked for a ride on it. The boy duly let him have it. Off he went down the street and the boy called out, 'Can I have my bike back?' Tommy shouted back, 'No! I'm keeping it!' and pedalled a bit further before turning around to give it back. That was outside Old Trafford. He was a jester, Tommy."

"We've got a photograph of you doing the same thing to us, Grandad," laughed Hannah. "Look, here it is."

"Ha! I remember that," said Terry. "That was the day you had us traipsing all over the place watching you horse riding."

"Y'know, a strange thing about all the lads who got killed, was that each one of them was the only boy in his family, no brothers. Eddie the same, and me, too, no brothers. Maybe that was part of what made us all so close. We were brothers on the pitch."

"They all look so young in the photos, Grandad," said Imogen.

"That's because they were. At the time, I was only 19 myself."

"There's only three photos left in this cluster," said Hannah. "Who else, Grandad?"

"This good-looking fella is Mark Jones," said Terry. "Notice how they all had proper haircuts. Clean cut lads. That was the discipline we all had from United. No scruffy shirts or shoes. No matter which team or which level we represented, we were Manchester United. Mark was a tough, powerful centre half, built like a rock. He gave no quarter on the pitch, but was an absolute gent off it. He's another with connections to Barnsley. That area produced loads of good footballers. His dad was a miner. Matt had six sisters, he was the third child of the seven. In his early time with United, he worked as a bricklayer around his hometown in Barnsley, which did him no harm in developing his strength and stamina levels. For most of the fifties he was the club's first choice centre half, and like some of the others we've talked about, he picked up two league title medals, he missed the Aston

Villa Cup Final with an eye injury, but he also helped the side to the semi-finals of the European Cup. He turned out 120 times for Manchester United, 103 of them in the league, a bit of an ever-present. He got picked just once for the England squad as a substitute, but never got on the pitch for them. Many folk said he would have gone on to a big international career if he hadn't died in Munich. He played in the same era as the great Billy Wright, so that kinda held back the playing opportunities for England early on. He left behind his wife, June, and their two-year old son, Gary. His daughter, Lynne, was born four months after Mark passed away. Gary had a trial with the club in the early seventies, but wasn't taken on at the time. Mark used to smoke a pipe, and we nicknamed him 'Dan Archer', after the pipe-smoking habit of that character in the radio serial, The Archers. Busby knew he smoked and always had his pipe with him, but Matt never made an issue of it. Mark's girlfriend used to sing down at the Ritz. Myself, Mark and Wilf McGuinness used to hang around the place together after training in the evenings. The high glamour life of a footballer, eh?"

"I bet you enjoyed, it though, Grandad?" said Imogen.

"We did enjoy it. Simple pleasures, great pals, what's to beat it?" said Terry.

He lifted the second last photograph from the table.

"Geoff Bent, this one," said Terry. "He was a no-nonsense, hard defender, and basically was cover for Roger Byrne on the left side and big Bill Foulkes on the right. He was aboard the flight as a possible stand-in for Roger, who'd been nursing a leg injury. In the event, Roger played and Geoff didn't get a game, but he was a solid Reds man. Many clubs came looking to sign him away from Old Trafford, but he chose to stay with us. Geoff was another son of a miner, and was born in Salford. He was the only child of Clifford and Clara Bent. United signed him as an apprentice when he left school in 1948, and he had several seasons playing in the youth and reserve sides, a great breeding ground for footballers. Over a few seasons, he had infrequent appearances in the first team, the first time in the 1954-55 campaign, mostly as cover for the other two established full backs. He and his wife had a baby daughter, Karen, who was only five months old at the time of the crash."

Terry put the photograph down and reached for the remaining one.

"Our man from Dublin, Liam Whelan," said Terry. "A gifted inside forward. Like so many of United's good players back then, they all knew how to get goals. They had flair, all of them, but this lad had tons of it. In 79 league matches for the club he scored 43 goals, better than one every two games. Over four seasons, that total grew with cup games and others to 52 goals. In the 1956-57 season, he became United's top scorer with 26 goals. Liam was part of a large family, but his father died when the boy was only eight years old. He was playing for an Irish club, Home Farm, in Whitehall, Dublin when he signed for United. He picked up one league title medal and helped them to the semi-finals of both the European Cup and the FA Cup. He also appeared four times for his country, the Republic of Ireland. It was well known that Liam was a staunchly religious Catholic.

For example, if he missed the morning mass on a Wednesday, he would ask Matt Busby if it was okay to go to church. The boss always let him attend. He wasn't a confident flyer, and the story goes that when the plane was revving up for the third take-off, Liam said, 'I'm ready to meet my Maker, I don't know about you lot, but if this is the time, then I'm ready.' He was an exceptional gentleman. The Irish national postal body, An Post, issued a postage stamp for the 50th anniversary of the Munich air disaster in 2008, showing an image of Liam. Further commemoration came in 2006, when a railway bridge in Dublin, near Dalymount Park was renamed in his honour. The Dublin City Council sanctioned the renaming of the bridge, which is also close to St. Attracta Road, the place where he was born. He's buried in Glasnevin Cemetery. His Manchester United team mate at the time of the crash, Sir Bobby Charlton, performed the unveiling ceremony."

"There's a huge fan support for United in Ireland, right, Grandad?" said Imogen.

"There's a huge support for the club worldwide, love," said Terry. "In fact, I'm told it's the most popular football club on the planet, not just in Ireland, but you're right, there's always been a massive following from across the Irish Sea."

He sat back, and was quiet. The photographs sprawled less tidily across the table than when they first began the afternoon. He reached forward, gathering them into a neat pile, and turned them face down. The girls knew he was thinking what to tell them next, and they stayed quiet also.

Then he spoke again, softly.

"Y'know, there were so many family members touched by the loss of these men, some only boys, really," he said. "The fans and the communities grieved for their loss of course, and that was real, but nothing will ever come close to what these families felt. The wives, the parents, the children, and the close friends who would never see them or speak with them again. It always seems more tragic when young people are killed, although, of course, anybody being killed is tragic. But they all died in their prime. It was a defining moment for Manchester as a community, and for United as a club. Anyone who knew anything about football and sport was affected emotionally one way or another. People who didn't know these lads personally still felt the tragedy. It was a dark, solemn time for everybody.

At the ground at Old Trafford, thousands gathered and wept openly. Schools were closed. The entire club was in mourning, as you can imagine. The memorial services and tributes weren't confined to Manchester. They took place all over Europe. It was a strange emotion. So many people who didn't know each other, united by the link of respect for those who died. Not just the players, of course. 15 others were also killed, including the co-pilot, journalists and club back room staff. It was the biggest single tragedy in the history of English football. Manchester United had almost been wiped out. But, as you both know, history shows us it was just the beginning of a rebirth."

Terry's eyes were more than moist. He knuckled his eyelids, as the girls gave him a group hug.

"Let's call a halt today" he said. "The next time with the others, we'll cover the boys who thankfully did survive. Okay?"

"Okay, Grandad," said Hannah. "They'll be ready."

6 THE REDS WHO SURVIVED

Terry put aside his newspaper at the sound of Phoebe and Trudy arriving.

"Hi, Grandad," said Trudy, embracing him.

"Hi, love. How are we doing?"

"Great," said Phoebe, butting in across them both. "We've got your stories about the players who died in the plane crash. Hannah said you'd tell us about the others today, right?"

"Right," said Terry. "There's a few of them, so let's not hang about."

The pile of photographs from the previous meeting were tidied at the far corner of the table. A different set of black and white images were arranged in a rainbow curve nearest where they sat.

"Y'know, I've been thinking about each of them again, and it struck home to me that some were so affected, they never played again, and some who did play never reached again the level they did before Munich. Not surprising really. It made me wonder what I would have done if I'd been on the plane and made it out alive."

"Oh, Grandad!" cried Trudy, jumping up and hugging him fiercely. "That's awful!"

"Time and place and all that, eh? Anyway, here's another bunch of good pals. This one's big Bill Foulkes."

"He looks like a really tough guy," said Trudy.

"None tougher, my love," said her grandad. "That man was made out of rock, I'm sure of it. He'd been with United since signing on from Whiston Boys club in 1950. He was the old-fashioned type of hard defender. He preferred playing at centre half, but Matt Busby sometimes had him playing at full back. During his footballing apprenticeship, he worked part time in the coal mine, believing, wrongly, that he might not be good enough to make the grade at a professional level in football. That idea was knocked out of him when he began to appear regularly for the senior team. His first game, funnily enough, was against Liverpool, and United won 2 -1, so a flying start against the old rivals."

"I read that he had a lucky escape from the crash," said Trudy.

"The way Bill tells it, he was more than just lucky," said Terry. "When the plane came to a halt after smashing into the fence and the hut, it broke apart right under his feet. The only injury he had was when a bottle of gin fell down from the locker above him and hit him on the head. He undid his safety belt and ran as fast as he could away from the crash, about 50 yards."

"Then what?" asked Phoebe.

"He realised the plane wasn't gonna explode, so he sprinted back to see if he could help anybody else to get out. From where he stood, he saw the tail end of the plane was on fire. There were some bodies still inside. Roger Byrne was still belted into his seat, and Bobby Charlton was in another seat, not moving at all. Harry Gregg was already back there, and they both tried to see what they could do to help. They didn't realise until the next morning that so many of their buddies had been killed."

"How horrible," said Phoebe. "You said he and Harry Gregg went back into the plane? How brave."

"Aye, love. More than brave, if y'ask me. Here's Harry's picture."

The fresh face of the Irish goalkeeper beamed from the photograph.

"On the night, there was a lot of panic and also a lot of courage," said Terry. "Harry is known everywhere as the reluctant hero of Munich. He went back in, time after time, to get people out of the wreckage. Remember, these guys had no way of knowing whether or not that plane would explode at any minute. Harry pulled out Jackie Blanchflower, Dennis Viollet, and Bobby Charlton. He also rescued a Yugoslavian diplomat's pregnant wife, Vera Lukic, and her daughter."

"Had Harry been very long at the club at the time?" asked Trudy.

"Only about three months. He transferred to United from Doncaster Rovers for a world record fee for a goalkeeper at £23,000, hardly the price of a current-day player's golf club fees! He ended up playing nearly 250 times for the club, and he's reckoned to be one of the greatest goalies we ever had. But for my money, what he did on the night of the crash was priceless."

"What happened to Bill Foulkes and Harry Gregg after that terrible night?" asked Phoebe.

"Great question, love. Harry continued playing for United until he was transferred to Stoke City in 1966. He was very unlucky with injuries in his playing career, and missed out on medals along the way. Bill Foulkes fared a bit better. Immediately after the crash, he took over the captaincy from the late Roger Byrne. He went on to play 688 games for United. He and Bobby Charlton were in the side in 1968 that won the European Cup for United for the first time. After his retirement, he remained as youth team coach, and parted company with the club in 1975, after 25 years of continuous service."

"You know a lot about these players, Grandad," said Phoebe. "How do you remember it all?"

"Ha, I have trouble remembering what day it is sometimes now, though! It's not too hard. When you play alongside men like them, you get to know just about everything there is to know about each other in the squad. And afterward, well, Manchester United has a strong tradition of family. That's what we were, even from the youth team onward. Family. What happened to them all later, was just like keeping up with family news."

"That makes sense," said Trudy.

"Your Grandad always makes sense," said Terry. "Didn't you know that?"

The big smiles were back on the face of the girls and their grandad. He laid out another trio of pictures.

"These three lads were all wingers. Johnny Berry, Albert Scanlon and Ken Morgans. At the time, they were 31, 22, and 18 years old respectively. The oldest, Johnny Berry, unfortunately, never played again after the crash. The second one, Albert, had terrible head injuries but the lad recovered from that, and had a good career for many years afterward. He scored 16 goals in the season following Munich. Gutsy, that. The last, Kenny, used to be a very quick winger, full of tricks, confident as anything, but he never seemed to get his form back after that night."

"That's a shame," said Phoebe.

"Yep. Johnny came to United from Birmingham City in 1951. He was a natural right winger, with great technique and speed, a classic Manchester United kinda winger. Even from the wing, he scored 44 goals in 277 games for the club. He won three league championships with us. Coincidentally, his starting place was being taken more often by young Kenny Morgans in a sort of changing of the guard. When he came out of the plane crash, he had no awareness of it, suffering a form of amnesia. It was only about four weeks afterward he found out by reading a newspaper article about it. The poor man had a lot of injuries that kept him in hospital for more than two months. He had a fractured skull, and broke his jaw, elbow, pelvis and one of his legs."

"TMI, Grandad," said Trudy.

"TMI, you what?"

"Too much information!"

"Maybe you're right, love. The human body can take a lot, but mentally I think it was too much to even think of playing again for Johnny," said Terry. "Whereas Albert Scanlon and Ken Morgans did play again, but with different degrees of success. Albert appeared for United at the start of the next season and played almost every game, scoring those 16 goals in the process. On the other hand, Ken never recovered the sort of sparkle his early skill had promised. Albert was a nephew of a former United winger, Charlie Mitten, and signed professionally for the club in 1952. He had a solid progression through the youth ranks, where I played in the same side with him a lot."

"What about Ken Morgans?" said Trudy. "When did he come to United?"

"As I remember, he joined straight from school when he was 16, and captained the winning FA Youth Cup team in 1957. When he was only 18, he made his first team debut versus Leicester City. It wasn't long before he was the first choice on the right wing. Quite miraculously, he was left unconscious during the crash, and he lay in the wreckage for five hours afterward. He was discovered by a couple of journalists after the official search had been called off."

"Wow!" said Phoebe. "That really is a miracle."

"It wasn't his time, love," said Terry. "But, as I said, he never really got back to playing the way he was before the crash."

Terry picked up his mug and pretended to peer into it with one eye closed.

"I think there's a hole in the bottom of this thing," he said. "D'you think somebody could rustle up another brew?"

"Me, Grandad!" shouted Phoebe, grabbing his mug. "Hang on."

While Phoebe went to the kitchen, her grandad returned the photographs of the three wingers to the table and picked out two more images.

When they were all settled in again, he said, "This is Ray Wood and Jackie Blanchflower."

The girls peered at the photographs in front them.

"Ray was another in the line of legendary goalkeepers to wear the number one shirt for United. He was between the sticks for the league-winning sides in 1956 and 1957. He was like a cat. Agile and quick. They say he was good enough to be a professional sprinter but he preferred football. When he was only 23 he was picked to play for England. He had really bad luck in the 1957 FA Cup Final against Aston Villa. In a clash with one of their forwards, he broke his jaw and had to be replaced in goal by Jackie Blanchflower, as there were no substitutes allowed in those days. He came back on the field and played in the forward line until the end of the game."

"That must have been painful," said Trudy.

"It was part and parcel of being a player in the fifties, love. Could you imagine a goalie doing that in the modern-day game? He suffered minor injuries in the crash, but only played one more first team game for United before being sold a year later to Huddersfield. He spent seven years with them, then one year with Bradford City, and ended his career after two years with Barnsley. The guy who went into goal in the Cup final when Ray was hurt, Jackie Blanchflower, had horrendous injuries in Munich. His pelvis was fractured and so were his legs and arms. His kidneys were severely crushed and he almost lost his right arm. He retired from football in 1959, having played his last game when he was just 24 years old."

Terry took a couple of sips from the mug of tea, and put it back down on the table. He retrieved the second last photograph from the row.

"Dennis Viollet, one of the lads that Harry Gregg brought out of the plane wreckage. Dennis joined United in 1949 and went through the usual process from the youth teams upward. He became a professional footballer a year after signing and got his first outing with the senior team in 1953, against Newcastle United. He played in the inside left position in the forward line, and excelled alongside Tommy Taylor. Nobody looked less like a dynamic player than Dennis. He was skinny, almost a bit underfed, but he was a goal machine. He set a club record for scoring in one season with 32 goals in 36 games in 1959-1960. In his time with United, he netted 179 goals in 293 matches. He knocked in four goals in the 10 – 0 victory over Anderlecht in the European Cup preliminary round in September, 1956. That score line still stands as United's record in the tournament. When he left the club in 1962, he signed for Stoke City, and carried on his playing career with them for another five years."

Terry picked up the remaining photograph.

"I think you know who this is, right?"

"Bobby Charlton," said Trudy. "Everybody in the world knows Bobby Charlton!"

"Ahem," roared Phoebe. "You mean, 'Sir Bobby Charlton'. Don't leave out the 'Sir' at the front!"

Trudy and her grandad laughed.

"You're dead right, love," said Terry. "Sir Bobby. And I can't think of a more well-deserved knighthood for one of the game's all-time gentlemen. What a player. Even in the youth team, we could tell he was destined to go all the way to the top. He had energy to burn in the middle of the field. His trademark was the ability to score goals from distance. I don't know to this day how he managed to get such power into his long-range shots, but he got some terrific goals from 'way outside the penalty area. Even if a goalkeeper was expecting his shots, he hit them so hard, it was often impossible for them to move in time to save them. Joe Armstrong has to be credited with bringing him to United. He saw him playing for East Northumberland Schools and signed him up on January 1st, 1953, when he was only fifteen, at the same time as my pal, Wilf McGuinness, who was also just fifteen.

Babes, indeed. Another wee bit of trivia for you is that his mother was not too keen to let him rely on a professional football career, so she had him start training as an apprentice electrical engineer. He turned professional in 1954, and the football world has been grateful for that ever since."

"More tea, Grandad?" said Phoebe.

"Not unless you've got more of those chocolate biscuits to go with it," he said.

"Coming up, right away," she said.

A few minutes later, with mugs refilled, Terry continued.

"Bobby was becoming a fixture in the side when Munich happened. He'd scored in the match in Belgrade. Over the years, he held lots of records which stood for a long time."

"Such as?" asked Trudy.

"For a start, he was United's leading goal scorer with 249 goals until Wayne Rooney passed that mark. He also held the same record for England with 49 goals, until Rooney, again, managed to surpass that number in September 2015. At United, he held the record for most appearances for the club, with 758 until Ryan Giggs topped that in the Champions League Final in Moscow against Chelsea in 2008."

"The Champions League took over from the old European Cup, right, Grandad?" said Phoebe.

"TMI! Ha, got you!" said Terry. "But you're right again, love. Bobby also had most games for England, at 106, before Bobby Moore and Peter Shilton overtook him. Don't forget, he was also in the team that won the World Cup in 1966. His brother Jack, played centre half in that final, too. In 1968, he was captain for Manchester when they beat Benfica 4 – 1 after extra time. Bobby scored twice in that match. As I said before, it was great playing with him in the early days with the youth team and so on. For a player like me, serving up from the wing, knowing people like Duncan Edwards and Bobby were getting on the end of your crosses and passes was magical. Great memories."

Terry had gone quiet again. The girls understood that would be the end of that day's session.

"Okay, Grandad," said Trudy. "We'll see you in the meeting after next. Love you."

"Love you, too," he said, leaning forward in his chair to take their hugs and goodbye kisses.

7 COACHING THE REDS

The interchange sessions with the pairs of granddaughters was working well. Everybody had done their homework on the previous meetings and prepared the follow-on sets of questions for their grandad.

Hannah and Imogen settled in their chairs, the notebooks on the table, with their handwriting showing some underlined questions in each of them. Terry was biting into his favourite sandwich, a sausage butty.

"That year, 1958, after February, must have been strange for everybody at the club, Grandad?" said Hannah.

"Yes, it took a long while to get back any sense of normality around the place," said Terry. "We came in as usual every day and carried on training. The balance of the season's matches continued like before, but of course, we all missed the lads who had been taken."

"You also joined the Army during that year, didn't you?" said Hannah.

"Near the end of that time, I did, yes," said Terry. "It wasn't so much joining as being called up."

"What do you mean, 'called up'?" asked Imogen.

"You're too young to know, love, but back in the day, every young fella was likely to be asked by his country to do National Service, being in the armed forces for a minimum of two years. It could be the Army, the Navy, or the Royal Air Force. I joined the Army. Weren't they lucky!"

"Oh, my God!" said Imogen. "Were you fighting people and shooting guns at them and stuff?"

Her grandfather laughed and shook his head.

"No, love. Thank God, I never ever fired a gun at anybody, but we were on active duty and we had to be ready for that if needed. I was stationed in Northern Cyprus for two years, and at the time there was a really bitter conflict going on between the Greeks in Southern Cyprus and Turkey, about who owned Northern Cyprus. I remember having nightmares when I returned there for a holiday with your Nana, thinking I would never be able to leave. I remember being hid in the streets of Nicosia, hiding in shadows with a fully armed gun. One night there was a lot of shooting and a horrible sight we found when we ran to help those wounded. Anyway, you don't need to hear more about that. You know, my Mam asked the radio to play my favourite song of the time and they did so we could hear it out there. People did that you see, as letters would take so long to reach you, if at all."

Terry rummaged through a sheaf of papers and assorted photographs at the far end of the table and picked out a black and white image to show the girls.

"There's me as a soldier, off to defend my Queen and Country. I bet she slept easy in her bed knowing that Private Beckett was in Her Majesty's Army."

Terry meeting the Shah of Persia

"I'm sure she did," said Hannah. "You mentioned going overseas with the Army. Where was that?"

"As I said, I went out to Cyprus with the Lancashire Fusiliers. The weather was magnificent. The island is slap bang in the middle of the Mediterranean, where everybody wants to go on holiday now. The fitness training was as good as at any of the league clubs. We played a lot of football. I represented the Army in various places out there."

"Anywhere fancy, Grandad?" asked Imogen.

"A few spots that might be a bit commonplace to visit nowadays, but the in the late fifties, they were considered quite exotic. Places like Turkey, Abadan and Iran. I met the Shah of Persia there. The country started to change some years later and eventually was subjected to the Iranian Revolution in 1979."

"Were you flying everywhere?" said Hannah.

"Mostly. When we flew back from Iran, part of the route for the plane was over Russia. That meant the flight had to get to a certain height above the country. We had to wear oxygen masks, which was unusual for us, but the Air Force boys were well used to it."

"Why the oxygen masks?" asked Imogen.

"Unlike today, the cabins weren't pressurised then," said Terry. "As a novelty, it was actually quite fun. We enjoyed travelling to play for the forces. I got to meet and team up with a lot of good lads. Many of them were already signed with various clubs across the country, and a few who weren't were also fine players. The military sides didn't get beaten very often. Fit as butcher's dogs, we were. Here's the medal I got."

"What did you get that for?"asked Imogen.

"Her Royal Majesty, the Queen, sent it especially for me for being the best ever football player in the Army," said Terry, with a straight face.

Imogen stared at him for a few moments, not knowing what to believe, until Hannah burst out laughing.

"Oh, Grandad!" said the younger girl, aiming one of her trademark play punches at Terry.

"How often did you get to come home from Cyprus?" asked Hannah.

"Only once from Cyprus. In the meantime, I began to suffer a series of niggling back injuries. That began to affect my football, as you can imagine. When I finished my time in the Army and came back home to Manchester, I was invited back to Old Trafford, but the back problems became too much and it never really worked out again after that."

"Do you want to talk about the coaches and managers for the Reds?" said Hannah, ticking the question on the page.

"Sure," said Terry. "You can have all the best players in the world in your club, but unless you coach and manage them properly, it amounts to nothing. That's why you see modern football managers getting paid absolute fortunes compared to all those years ago. In our day, they were in it as much for the love of the game than anything else. It's common knowledge that United's history is steeped in youth football. You've seen it with the Busby Babes, and later with Sir Alex Ferguson's sides. The Manchester United Academy has been a terrific source of talent. But it takes more than raw talent to make it to the top and be part of a great club philosophy. That's where the training and motivation comes in, getting young kids to channel their skills to express their talent without fear. Of course, there are systems to follow, but nothing beats that glorious burst of movement when a player does his own thing, the individual stuff that makes the fans roar. The club has long since prided itself in investing in the youth and junior teams. It wasn't long before other clubs picked up on the idea, seeing how effective it was for United. Some great, world-class footballers came out of the Academy and Reserves."

Press Photo–Kemsley Newspapers Limited
Manchester United Junior Team
Photograph taken 15th August 1955 prior to the Public Practise Match
Blues v Reds at Old Trafford.
Standing: Beckett, Dawson, Hawksworth, Fulton, Birkett, Beswick
Sitting: Pearson, Yauld, Colman, P. Jones, Hall.

"All local players, Grandad?" asked Imogen.

"Well, if you count Georgie Best being from Northern Ireland as almost local, United Kingdom, that is, yes, home-grown and developed players. It's hard to beat a list that includes Duncan Edwards, Eddie Colman, and Bobby Charlton from my time. Add in later, guys like Bestie, David Beckham, Gary Neville, Paul Scholes, and Ryan Giggs, who was called Ryan Wilson, by the way, when he first came to United. All of these lads played for United in the Youth Cup like we did. No wonder the club has been the most successful in that tournament. You have to say the coaching at that level has been consistently outstanding. United has had many excellent coaches over the years, but for me, two names stand out, apart from Matt Busby himself. Jimmy Murphy and Eric Harrison."

Terry paused and held out his empty mug. Hannah filled it this time.

"Jimmy Murphy's contribution to United is as much as anybody's who was ever associated with the club. Especially after the Munich crash. But his influence began long before that. He was actually Welsh, born in Ton Pentre in South Wales. Like a lot of great coaches, he also played the game professionally at the highest level, up until the start of the Second World War, turning out more than two hundred times for West Bromwich Albion and fifteen times for his country. When the war was over, Matt Busby brought Jimmy to the club as chief coach. It happened by coincidence that Busby was in the audience when Jimmy gave a talk on football to a group that was made up mainly of young conscripted soldiers. Matt was so impressed, he snapped up Jimmy's services at the first opportunity. He had such a huge impact on us as youngsters, and even the seasoned professionals followed his discipline. In fact, later he was responsible for getting Wales into the World Cup Finals, the last time they ever got that far."

"He must have been a bit special," said Imogen.

"More than just a bit, love," said Terry. "I don't know if part of it was his Welsh upbringing, but he was a powerful motivator, an emotional man, and totally committed to the club. He understood Matt Busby's desire to build the best youth set-up of any football club, anywhere, and my, he did just that. Matt and Jimmy were a formidable team together."

"Like Butch Cassidy and the Sundance Kid, Grandad?" asked Hannah, laughing.

"I don't know about that, love, but everybody knew about Busby and Murphy," said her grandad. "I know Sir Alex Ferguson said he wished he'd had more time to listen to Jimmy over the years. And Nobby Stiles said there wouldn't have been a Manchester United if it wasn't for Jimmy Murphy. He reckoned Jimmy liked him, because Nobby always got stuck in, no holds barred on the pitch. When Albert Scanlon came to the club, he was petrified of Murphy. He demanded you gave everything on the field, nothing left on there when you came off after playing, and who's to say he was wrong? We won more than we lost or drew, at all levels."

"What made him so special?" asked Imogen.

"Apart from his depth of knowledge about how the game should be played? Remember, he'd been a terrific player himself. But I think it was that he cared so much for each of us. He knew everything about us, what made us tick as players. We were all number one to him. He took the reins of the club after the plane crash, truly an inspirational man at a time that true inspiration was needed. He told us the club would not be bowed by the tragedy. That we would show the world what United were, and that how we behaved then would shape what we would be in the future. He was the right man at the right time for Manchester United after Munich."

"You mentioned Eric Harrison," recalled Hannah.

"Eric was later, of course. He joined the club in 1981 as youth manager when Ron Atkinson was in charge. He worked well with the younger lads, and propelled Norman Whiteside to the upper ranks. Norman became a superstar with the club. After 1986, when Sir Alex took over, he kept Eric in his job, looking after the younger talent. Nobody can argue against the success he created then. You can reel off the names and everybody in football knows who they are. David Beckham, Paul Scholes, Ryan Giggs, Nicky Butt, and Gary Neville. Legends, love. Legends. Here, get us another brew, somebody. I think that's enough for today, right? When Trudy and Phoebe come next time, I'll talk about a bit about Sir Matt Busby."

"Oh, Grandad, can we all come for that one?" said Hannah. "We all want to listen to you about Sir Matt."

Terry chuckled.

"Okay, I should sell tickets for it, if the four of you are coming, right?"

"Right, Grandad, thanks" said Hannah. "See you tomorrow."

8 SIR MATT BUSBY

There was plenty of room at the table, even with the four girls, and Terry himself comfortably placed in the middle chair.

"I must say, I'm honoured to have such a fabulous audience," said Terry, pretending to speak into an invisible microphone.

"Stop kidding, Grandad," said Hannah. "We're really keen to learn from you about Sir Matt."

"Well, as usual, your old Grandad has also done his homework," he said.

"I'm going to give you a lot of background and history about him."

"Yay!" said Phoebe.

"First up, as I've said before, back in the old days, the best managers and coaches were footballers themselves at one time or another. They really understood the game inside out. Matt was no different in that way."

"Did he play for United?" asked Imogen.

"Nearly," said Terry. "When he was playing for Manchester City in 1930, he was offered to the club, but the asking price of £130 was more than they could afford to pay. Can you believe that? Although he was Scottish, like Sir Alex Ferguson, his family lived in Manchester. He signed for City in 1928, when he was 18, and earned the princely sum of £5 per week. At the time of his signing, the contract allowed for him to leave at the end of it to emigrate to America as the family had planned. He decided to stay, and made his first team debut appearance on November 1929. He started off as an inside forward, but was soon moved back into the right half back position, where his positional play, superb passing skill and football intelligence were better used. He appeared in two Cup Finals with City, winning one, and losing the other. In all, he played more than 200 times for City before being sold to Liverpool in 1936 for £8,000. He was made Liverpool captain and played for them for three seasons."

"Why only three seasons, Grandad?" said Trudy.

"Because the war started in 1939, love, and that disrupted everything and everybody. Matt joined up in the Army, like most of the Liverpool playing staff, enlisting in the King's Liverpool Regiment. During the war, he played for teams where he could, as did many of the lads. He turned out at different times for clubs like Chelsea, Reading, Brentford, Middlesbrough, Bournemouth and Hibernian in Edinburgh. His solo appearance in the full England team was in 1933, but during the war he was picked in unofficial internationals for England seven times, all of them against his own country, Scotland."

"How did he become a manager?" asked Hannah.

"During the war, he was a football coach for the Army's Physical Training Corps. After the war, Liverpool gave him an offer to come and be their assistant team coach. However, he asked for control of the first team and they didn't want to give him that at the time. He let the offer pass. In the meantime, Louis Rocca, the famous United scout, had become a good friend. To cut a long story short, Louis intervened with the club's Chairman, James W. Gibson, recommending that Matt be hired. Busby was adamant that he needed to be in control of picking the players the club bought and sold, especially choosing the team for the match days, and to be involved in the training. That last bit, about the training was the foundation of what United was later to become in terms of the youth policy and the great playing style that developed though the next several years. He started as manager in October 1945. He served the club for a quarter of a century and amassed 13 trophies in that reign. Only Sir Alex has delivered more than that. The club has been blessed with two of the greatest football managers that ever lived."

"What was he like to work with?" said Imogen.

"A marvellous boss and a great man, love," said Terry. "I've met Sir Alex many times, of course, but not ever in a working relationship as we did with Sir Matt. We were like sons to him. He believed a million percent in each of us. It's no accident that he was the one who brought through from the lower levels into the first team guys like Duncan, Bobby, Liam Whelan, Albert Scanlon, Bill Foulkes, Jackie Blanchflower, David Pegg, and Mark Jones. He was very clever early in his management when he brought aboard Jimmy Murphy. I talked about Jimmy last time with you two girls, right?'

"Right, Grandad," said Imogen. "We shared it with Trudy and Phoebe last night."

"Okay, well time to do some more sharing. How about finding us another brew? Don't hang about! And I think there's more Vimto for you in the kitchen as well."

When everyone settled down, Terry began again.

"On top of the youngsters I mentioned already, he transferred in Harry Gregg, Tommy Taylor and the older Johnny Berry. They were all delighted to join the club family, and fitted in terrifically with the set-up. Under Matt's management, United were placed second in the league in 1946-47, '48, '49, and '51 and won it in 1952, as well as being FA Cup Final winners in 1948."

"What sticks in your mind about him when you were in the youth team, Grandad?" asked Hannah.

"Y'know, he wasn't a loud man. Hardly ever raised his voice. He never seemed to get rattled or visibly upset about things. That kinda translated into all of us, and I'm sure at the first team level as well. They say the same thing about Fergie. Great man-management skills. I do remember very clearly his habit at half time. In the dressing-room he would tell us exactly how we were playing. As we made our way back out he had individual words for each of us, just a sentence or a word or two of encouragement and guidance."

"Such as?" said Phoebe.

"Wee things, really. He might say, 'keep out on the wing a bit more', or 'press the fullback on the inside, he's a bit weak there.' Stuff like that. He was an insightful manager and knew what he was talking about. Nobody was treated differently from anybody else around him in the club. He treated us all with the same respect. Of course, we adored the man. Sometimes when we went to Blackpool with the first team, he would take us to what was called then the Norbreck Castle Hotel for training outside on the beach. They would give us some spending money and we'd go along to the amusements and enjoy the afternoon. Great times."

"He almost never made it back from Munich, right, Grandad?" said Trudy.

"He had horrific injuries from the crash, not only physically, but the mental pain of losing all the young men under his care was a terrible burden to him for a long time afterward. He was given the last rites twice, as they thought he wouldn't pull through. He spent nine weeks in the hospital. For the first couple of weeks they didn't dare tell him that Edwards had passed away, as they thought that might be the last straw for him then. Eventually, he asked a Franciscan friar how Duncan was doing, and the friar decided he should tell him. His wife, Jean, then told him of the other fatalities. It's common knowledge he told his wife he felt such guilt over the deaths and had lost the will to carry on managing the club. Thankfully for all concerned, she persuaded him to overcome that, in honour of those who had died. Jimmy Murphy had not been in Munich, and he looked after the team in Matt's absence. Busby was able to attend the FA Cup Final three months later, which United lost to Bolton Wanderers. Sit Matt passed away in 1988 at the age of 80. The coincidences in dates is quite strange. In 1999, United won the European Cup, on what would have been Sir Matt's 90th birthday, and the first time since his side did it in 1968. In 2008, United beat Chelsea in Moscow to win the Champions League, 40 years after Matt won it, and 50 years after Munich."

The girls began to chatter.

"Any more today, Grandad?" asked Imogen.

"Let's carry on next time," said Terry. "Who's coming?"

"Me and Phoebe," said Trudy.

"That means I've got to get in some more Vimto. Okay."

One by one, his granddaughters hugged and kissed him goodnight.

9 SCOUTING FOR THE REDS

"What are we going to talk about today, Grandad?" asked Phoebe. Three days had passed since the big session on Sir Matt Busby with all the girls present. Now, only Phoebe and her sister were catching up with Terry.

"Let's cover the scouting I did for the club, eh?" he said, flexing his fingers together until they made a cracking noise. "You remember earlier, I told you how important Joe Armstrong was to the club?"

"Yep. He came to talk to your mum and dad to get you to sign, right?" said Trudy.

"Exactly. Without guys like Joe, the club would've had no proper way of discovering new blood. Playing talent was everywhere in the country. In the schools, in the counties and so on, but scouts were important to find out which lads stood out from the rest."

"How did you get started?" asked Phoebe.

"I'd known Brian Kidd for a while, and when he took over the management of the youth team in 1981, he was looking for people to help sniff out new players for the Academy."

"Brian Kidd was part of the team that won the European Cup for United in 1968, wasn't he, Grandad?" said Trudy.

"He was, and he got the third goal in extra time, which knocked the stuffing out of Benfica. It was his nineteenth birthday that day. What a birthday present, eh? Anyway, he asked me to join the scouts and I was delighted to do that. Nobby Stiles was doing the same thing at the same time, but he later gave it away as he became very busy on the speaker circuit, talking at dinners and stuff."

"How long did you do it for?" said Phoebe.

"About thirty-two years, love. It was great to be still a part of the club. I would get up early on Saturdays, more on Sundays, and I was told which games to go and watch. I'd get my overcoat and a good 'fry up' and off I'd go, sometimes up on the hills on the borders of the Yorkshire Moors. I'd often see a City scout I became pals with, and we'd share a flask of hot coffee. We got to know each other, being at the same matches, week in week out. Sometimes he would point out a certain young lad, sometimes I'd single out another. There were lots of schools' association games, sometimes county matches. At the bigger gatherings, you would see many people watching on the side of the pitch, taking notes here and there, and you'd know they were scouts."

"You didn't know them all?" asked Trudy.

"Not all, no. But the regulars, yes. We'd chat sometimes. They were mostly decent guys. Doing the same thing as me. Like myself, some had played the game professionally, and their clubs relied on their judgement to bring in fresh, new players for them."

"How often were you able to spot players who were good enough to bring to United?" said Phoebe.

"You might be surprised, but I took a good few down to the Academy. Some stayed for years, of course, but never made it as far as the first team. That's only natural. But we kept a good pipeline going."

"Any big stars?" asked Phoebe.

"None of them were big stars at the time we brought them in, of course. That came later when they made the first team and international appearances. We could see the potential in a lot of these lads. That's what a scout is supposed to do. Spot the good ones early before other clubs grab them. There was a ton of competition, y'know."

"How young were these players?" said Trudy.

"For example, I brought in Paul Scholes when he was only thirteen, back in 1987. Even for a small lad, he was a dynamo in the middle of the park. He seemed to see things so much quicker than anybody else. Many years later, the great Zinedine Zidane said that Paul was probably the best midfielder he had ever seen. Scholesie was playing for Cardinal Langley RC High School when I first saw him. He was a natural."

"I remember my dad saying you took him to the barber in Middleton one summer and you were chatting with Paul Scholes," said Phoebe. "You only told him who he was when you were walking away."

"Yep, I remember your dad, Simon saying that," said Terry.

"Didn't Paul Scholes have to move house from Alkrington because he kept getting his washing stolen from the line?" said Trudy. "Is that true?"

"That's how the story goes," said her grandad. "I remember the first time Scholesie played for England. Me and your Nana were in Ireland on holiday, and he was all over the telly and the Manchester Evening News. He mentioned me and Mike Coffey from Cardinal Langley, saying thanks. Coffey was the deputy head and English teacher at the school. He used to teach your Mum and Auntie Nicola. He was a United scout too. By the way, the other Paul, your uncle, Hannah and Imogen's dad, has always been an avid red and your Auntie Nicola has been to many a match over the years, but Auntie Carol, Auntie Caroline, she used to come every week before going to university, they all knew her name down there."

"When you watched these boys at such a young level, what were you looking for that told you they would make good professional players?" asked Trudy.

"Y'know, that's the hardest thing to answer. You look for someone who stands out. But then again, being good enough for United is one thing, and standing out is somewhat different. Some lads are quite good, get to play with better players and end up learning things which brings them on. But it's a bit too much for others and they fail to develop. A player such as David Beckham, for example, was devout about the game. That is what you have to be. It's a thing you can't teach a child. The game has got to be the number one thing in their life. When Beckham, Butt and Scholes were young lads, I would see them kicking the ball around a long time after all the professionals had gone home. They were driven and focused. In all my years of scouting, and there are a few, I have never come across another Duncan Edwards."

"You also picked out Nicky Butt, right?"

"Nicky was even younger than Scholesie when I saw him play. He was only twelve. I knew he would play for England one day, and he did. What another fabulous servant he's been to United. He played for twelve years in the first team. He went back to the club as Academy manager in 2016. Nicky would always have time for a chat with me when I went down to the training ground at Carrington. A good bloke. The other players from that time also knew me, of course, and always had a nice word or two."

"You must have been at the training ground a lot over the years, Grandad," said Phoebe.

"Yep. I used to take Johnny Macken to the training in the mid-nineties, then drop him off at Plant Hill near Blackley on the way home. He never made the first team at United, but he went on to several other clubs, including Manchester City. He scored in the derby against United in 2004. After that, he had spells at Crystal Palace, Ipswich Town, Derby, and Barnsley. He also made one international appearance for Northern Ireland."

He handed his mug to Phoebe, for refilling.

"Thanks, love."

"As a scout, you were very much a part of the United set-up, right?" asked Trudy.

"A hundred percent," said Terry. "We were always invited to the cup finals. Sometimes we were flown down to London, other times we were in coaches and stopped on the way for meals in a stately home or big tents on the lawns. Once when we flew down, one of our planes had already landed, we were about to land next, so near the ground and then the pilot announced something and we went up again. My heart was in my mouth and we were circling for ages. Anyhow, we landed safely in the end. Another time, it was funny, we were approaching Wembley on the United coach and we saw your Mum, Clare, and Auntie Caz. Was it the treble year? I can't remember now. Your Mum was living in Harrow at the time, and I got them tickets for the cup final. I got the bus driver to stop and let them on. Everyone was excited. It was great to see them before the match as we were seated in a special bit, separate from them. There were about thirteen or fourteen buses from the club."

Manchester United Scouts with Sir Alex Ferguson

"You met Sir Alex a few times, too?" said Phoebe.

"Fergie is a great bloke. You know why? He always sat with us scouts and had a chat. He knew our names. The man is a class act. About twelve years back now, he said to me personally, 'You have two tickets for home matches for good.'"

" 'For good', what does that mean?"

"You know, forever. And he handed them to me for that season. He used to keep his players on track. One time, he heard the lads were at a party at a house in Salford. He got in his car and drove over and stormed in. Giggs was in his early twenties, and was hiding under the bed. Real discipline, that was. Another time he took the winger, Lee Sharpe, into his own house for a while. Sharpe was a bit of a lad, but Alex knew how to manage him."

"Did many of the players you brought to the club keep in touch with you?" said Phoebe.

"Lots of them. Your Nana and me were invited to players' weddings from time to time. And I've tried to follow where some went after they left United. To other clubs. I feel a part of their careers, and it's good to see them being successful, at United and elsewhere."

"We're nearly finished now, Grandad," said Trudy, closing her notebook.

"Hannah and Imogen will be here tomorrow for the last session. We think it would be great if you give us your opinions on comparing your playing days and what it's like nowadays. Okay?"

"Sounds like a plan," Terry affirmed. "Hugs please."

10 THEN AND NOW

Terry opened the door.

"There's the four of you again!" he said. "What's going on?"

"We decided at the last minute, we all wanted to be here because it's the final bit," said Hannah. "You don't mind, do you, Grandad?"

He laughed out loud.

"Mind? Why should I mind? I love you all the same, you know that! The more the merrier. Come on in and let's get started. Somebody get the tea ready. There's enough of you to handle that. I thought you'd be here a while ago."

"We were just finishing a game on the Xbox," commented Phoebe.

"Your generation play more football on the telly with that box thing than you do on the pitch. In the summer holidays I used to visit my cousins in South Manchester, well Cheshire, it was posh there. They lived in Style, near Quarry Bank Mill, loads of fields to run around in. We'd play football with their pals and they'd say 'don't tell the lads that you are playing with United', and we'd hammer them. They were always surprised at my skills, and we'd walk away laughing," remarked Terry.

"Cool," said Imogen."

"Do you want biscuits or a sausage butty, Grandad?" asked Trudy.

"Can't we have both in this house? Go on, don't hang about. Make us all a butty each if you like."

Imogen and Trudy, headed for the kitchen, while Hannah and Phoebe prepared the places at the table with all the notebooks ready.

A quarter of an hour later, with fingers cleaned from the butties, Hannah started the questions.

"What's the biggest difference from when you played?"

"They don't have Terry Beckett flying down the wing anymore," he said.

"Grandad!" Phoebe and Imogen cried in unison.

"I suppose the main difference is the amount of money that's in football now. It beggars belief, really. The television cash is in the billions. Transfer fees are ridiculous, and frankly, so are the wages the players are getting. To be honest, in my day, most of us would have played for United, even if they didn't pay us. Putting on that Reds' shirt was the most important thing for us. I don't begrudge the lads the money now, because that's what the public and the television companies are paying for. The advertisers foot the front money, and the man in the street still has the choice to buy the end product or not. I think they have to be a bit careful, though. Not all the clubs in the lower leagues are doing well financially, and that used to the prime source of the up and coming talent. All local."

"It's not local any more, is it, Grandad?" said Trudy.

"No, it's not. The world has become a much smaller place in that respect," said Terry. "With the money, the bigger clubs have networks and people all over the globe looking and searching for the best they can find and afford. We tended to be English, with a few Jocks and Welshmen. On the plus side, it gave United legends like Eric Cantona and Ronaldo. I'll have you a bet nowadays, most of the Premier League sides don't even have half of their first team as home-grown British. By the way, that goes for the coaches and managers as well.

Y'know, many of the United players were so well regarded locally, they now have streets named after them. For example, just from the Munich crash players alone, there's Roger Byrne Close, Tommy Taylor Close, the Eddie Colman Close, Billy Whelan Walk, the David Pegg Walk, the Mark Jones Walk, and the Duncan Edwards Court. Not so long ago, I was present when they unveiled the Nobby Stiles Drive. This terrific photograph came from our pals at the Manchester Evening News, always great supporters of United. I'm here at the far left. Included in that group are some magical footballing names to remember. Bobby Charlton, Denis Law, Johnny Giles, Carlo Sartori, Brian Kidd, and Alan Gowling. Not to be outdone, there's also a Sir Alex Ferguson Way in Stretford in Manchester."

"Sir Alex and Matt Busby are probably two of the greatest football managers the game has ever known, or ever will know. What they did at United was unbeatable. Busby in his own era, and in the modern day, Fergie is unmatched."

"Who was better?" said Imogen.

"Each was phenomenal, love. I think Fergie gets the vote because of all the titles he won. It's hard to see that ever being reached again. Talking about the coaches and managers, in the time of Jimmy Murphy and Sir Matt, they knew every player inside out. They worked with them on the training pitches every day. Nowadays, there's a whole back room team of trainers, specialists, masseurs, fitness and diet experts looking after the players. Of course, that brings another huge comparison. Many of these lads today are like pedigree horses. They're trained to a very high level, complete athletes now. I see players getting injured during the warm-up before games. That never happened when I played. I told you before, many of the lads even smoked openly back then, and lots of them certainly took a good drink, although most of that has been kicked into touch now, apart from a few incidents in nightclubs. Heck, we didn't make enough money to afford to go to night clubs! Speaking of drinks. How about another brew, please?"

Imogen took his mug.

"So what did you think of Jose Mourinho as a manager?" asked Hannah.

"Well, it appeared that he wasn't happy with United's transfer policy, but also the players didn't seem to gel with him. Now Ole Gunnar Solskjaer, he was always a lovely guy and a great player. It's 20 years since the treble and that amazing goal. You know, they were all boarding the bus once, the players. I had been getting signatures on a ball that was being auctioned for a charity but Ole was already sat down. You know, he got off the bus, signed it and wished me luck. He always came across as very calm, focused and positive - no drama. That's what makes a good leader. Hey, what was it like when you three young ones were at the match on Boxing Day against Huddersfield? That was a good game."

"It was amazing... 3-1 for United." said Imogen.

"There was near to 75,000 and the crowd in the Stretford end kept singing 'Ole, Ole Ole Ole'..." gasped Phoebe.

"Yep and 'Ole, Ole give us a wave', and he did. He hugged the mascot too. We were all singing. The fans like him for sure. It wasn't too cold either." said Trudy.

"Well, that's five games with him as caretaker manager and five wins. What a great start to 2019. It is a United legend returning and he is playing them by encourage the full-backs to push up the pitch which gives the game width. Here's to The Reds being top of the league again!" reflected Terry.

"It's a major change the way sides are set up to play today compared to my days. In the fifties and sixties, the formation was easy. A goalie, two fullbacks, three half backs and five forwards. 'Midfield' is a term that came much later on. When England beat Germany in the World Cup final at Wembley in 1966, the manager, Alf Ramsey, used what was known as a 4 - 4 - 2 formation. Kinda boring, to be honest, but effective when you have the right players following it. The downside is that less and less really fast wingers are used now.

Also, full backs sometimes behave like wingers themselves, becoming part of the attack."

"Who's the best player you've seen?" said Hannah.

"You've got it in the name right there, love. Best. George Best. People would pay money just to watch him do his stuff on the field. Fearless, a genius with a ball at his feet. They used to say with one swerve of his body, he could send the crowd the wrong way! But there were plenty of great players in my day. Eddie Colman, Bobby Charlton and lots of others. Later players I liked at United were Eric Cantona, Brian Robson, Scholes and Beckham. When Beckham concentrated on his football and not his hairstyle, he was much better in my opinion. I see the players today, some of them, spending as much money on how they look, rather than concentrating on how they play, and I wonder what Sir Matt would have thought of them. The other thing that's really changed is the way some players act like dying swans when they get tackled. Referees protect them far too much now. Men's football is for players, not ballet dancers. I'd like to see how some of the present divas would get on against guys like Dave Mackay, Billy Bremner, Ron Harris, Roy Keane and Vinnie Jones."

"Were they tough?" said Imogen, wide-eyed.

"I'd call them hard, but they played within the rules. Mostly."

Hannah smiled.

"One thing I do like to see, is football growing among girls like yourselves," said her grandad. "The more interest in the game the better. I'd love to see our Trudy and Phoebe here play for England one day. You two have played forever, travelling the Gulf and a fair few medals eh? Phoebe you were in the British Schools of the Middle East winning team this year, right? I remember Phoebe in her lessons sitting on the ball as a toddler and pulling the grass out of the ground, at least the other team couldn't score eh!"

"Yay!' said Imogen.

"We still get together you know, the old players" said Terry.

"Any more questions?" Hannah asked the rest of the girls. "If not, that's what they call 'a wrap', I think. Grandad, thanks ever so much for answering all our stuff."

"It's me that has to thank you lot. I've enjoyed every minute of it," said Terry. "It took me back, and I loved it. Now, who's got the tea?"

Frank Wilson

With Compliments From

 The Association of Former Manchester United Players 20th April 2012

Terry Beckett, front line, third from the right, with Alex Ferguson centre front

ABOUT THE AUTHORS

I'm Hannah. I am interested in fashion and inspired by those who are adventurous and not afraid to speak out. I am studying A levels and aspire to attend university in time. I want to become a teacher and also travel the world, this is a huge goal of mine.

Hannah Barbara Ann Moore

Hello, my name is Trudy. My favourite subjects are Drama and Art. I like playing football, singing and shopping for clothes. Long term I want to attend university in the UK and study Drama.

Trudy Kate Beckett-McInroy

Hi I'm Phoebe. My favourite subject as school is PE. I play football and athletics competitively. I also play the flute and games on-line. I love making slime and playing keepy-ups on my trampoline.

Phoebe Evangeline Beckett-McInroy

Hi my name is Imogen and my favourite subjects at school are Art and Maths. I am ten years old and love my horse riding lessons and playing the guitar. I am also enthusiastic about gymnastics and slime!

Imogen Nicola Moore

REFERENCES

Greenhalgh, S., (22 January 2008: Retrieved May 2018), Remembering a legend, Messenger Newspapers.

Dudley News, (30 January 2008), Duncan Edwards – 50 years on

Endlar, A., (Retrieved May, 2018), Mark Jones, StretfordEnd.co.uk

Endlar, A., (Retrieved May, 2018), Geoff Bent, StretfordEnd.co.uk

Gulf Weekly (2013: RetrievedMay 2018), An Eye For Talent, www.gulfweekly.com/Articles/31343//AN-EYE-FOR-TALENT

James, G., (2006). Manchester City - The Complete Record. Derby: Breedon. p. 341

Holt, Nick; Lloyd, Guy (2006). Total British Football. Flame Tree Publishing

Horne, John; Tomlinson, Alan; Whannel, Garry (1999), Understanding Sport: An Introduction to the Sociological and Cultural Analysis of Sport, Taylor and Francis

Leighton, James (2002). Duncan Edwards: The Greatest. London: Simon & Schuster UK

McCartney, Iain (2001). Duncan Edwards: The Full Report.Britespot Publishing Solutions

Matt Busby, (Retrieved May 2018), www.londonhearts.com, London Hearts Supporters' Club

Matt Busby, (Retrieved May 2018), www.scottishfa.co.uk

McCartney, I., (2000), Roger Byrne: Captain of the Busby Babes, Empire Publications Ltd

Murphy, A., (2006), The Official Illustrated History of Manchester United, London: Orion Books, pp. 62–63

Penney, I., (1995), The Maine Road Encyclopedia, Edinburgh: Mainstream, p. 37

Sir Matt Busby Profile, (Retrieved May 2018), Official Manchester United website - www.manutd.com

Ward, A., (1984). The Manchester City Story. Derby: Breedon. p. 32

White, J., (2008). Manchester United: The Biography. London: Sphere. p. 62.

LIST OF PHOTOGRAPHS

Photographs from Terrence Beckett's own personal collection. Every effort has been taken to trace any copyright holders and we apologise in advance for any unintentional omissions. We would be happy to insert the appropriate acknowledgements in future editions.

Printed in Great Britain
by Amazon